Praise for *Memoir as M*

"This is a book about plain, humble hum......

as an aside it teaches you how to write about such things effectively, but I think the book's power and ultimate purpose is to help the reader survive a normal human life, with all its absurdities and impossible challenges."

— **Thomas Moore**, author of *Care of the Soul* and *Soul Therapy*

"Nancy Aronie writes from a large heart and a powerful brain, which is why her new book is so quickly becoming an essential addition to fine literature. The work is a frontrunner, and so is she."

— **Robert S. Brustein**, theater critic, producer, playwright, educator, and founder of the Yale Repertory Theatre and the American Repertory Theater and Institute

"After reading the first few chapters of Nancy Aronie's *Memoir as Medicine*, all I wanted to do was write. Anyone struggling to stay with the process should read this book immediately! Aronie's practical advice and sense of humor will keep you going. The book is a treasure."

— **Mirabai Starr**, author of *Caravan of No Despair: A Memoir of Loss and Transformation* and *Wild Mercy: Living the Fierce and Tender Wisdom of the Women Mystics*

"The unqualified success of *Memoir as Medicine* lies in the authenticity of the author's voice. It's the best writing advice since Anne Lamott's *Bird by Bird*. Throughout the book, it's a pleasure to be in Nancy Aronie's wise company."

— **Wally Lamb**, author of *I Know This Much Is True* and five other *New York Times* bestsellers

"Nancy Aronie's disarmingly intimate, deeply insightful, uniquely funny, and profoundly moving book is a must-read! *Memoir as Medicine* unfolds in a myriad of unexpected ways...and yet somehow precisely reconnects us to our own personal quest for purpose, truth, and meaning."

— **Tony Shalhoub**, Screen Actors Guild, Golden Globe, Emmy, and Tony Award–winning actor

"At her famed workshops on Martha's Vineyard, Nancy Aronie is described as the midwife to her students' writing lives. Now she has brought forth a literary offspring of her own, pulsing with passion and pain, heart and hilarity."

— **Geraldine Brooks**, Pulitzer Prize–winning author of *March*, five bestselling novels, and three works of nonfiction

"If this book doesn't get you motivated, I don't know what will. Nancy Aronie gives perfect examples using her own gorgeous stories. You will laugh, you will probably cry, but I promise you, you will write!"

— **Carly Simon**, author and Grammy Award–winning singer-songwriter

"Moving, helpful, inspiring, and tender, *Memoir as Medicine* makes you want to get up off your butt and write the heart and soul of your life."

— **Jack Kornfield**, author of *A Path with Heart*

Memoir *as* Medicine

Also by Nancy Slonim Aronie

Writing from the Heart

Memoir *as*
Medicine

The Healing Power of Writing
Your Messy, Imperfect, Unruly
(*but Gorgeously Yours*) Life Story

NANCY SLONIM ARONIE

New World Library
Novato, California

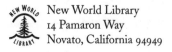 New World Library
14 Pamaron Way
Novato, California 94949

Text design by Tona Pearce Myers

Library of Congress Cataloging-in-Publication Data

Names: Aronie, Nancy Slonim, date, author.
Title: Memoir as medicine : the healing power of writing your messy, imperfect, unruly (but gorgeously yours) life story / Nancy Slonim Aronie.
Description: Novato, California : New World Library, [2022] | Summary: "A discussion of the healing benefits of memoir writing along with pragmatic advice for writing one. Includes a set of prompts, directions, and examples to help readers become writers of their own personal stories"-- Provided by publisher.
Identifiers: LCCN 2021057616 (print) | LCCN 2021057617 (ebook) | ISBN 9781608688074 (paperback) | ISBN 9781608688081 (epub)
Subjects: LCSH: Autobiography--Authorship. | Authorship--Therapeutic use. | Autobiographical memory.
Classification: LCC PE1479.A88 A76 2022 (print) | LCC PE1479.A88 (ebook) | DDC 808.06/692--dc23/eng/20211124
LC record available at https://lccn.loc.gov/2021057616
LC ebook record available at https://lccn.loc.gov/2021057617

First printing, March 2022
ISBN 978-1-60868-807-4
Ebook ISBN 978-1-60868-808-1

Printed in Canada on 100% postconsumer-waste recycled paper

 New World Library is proud to be a Gold Certified Environmentally Responsible Publisher. Publisher certification awarded by Green Press Initiative.

10   9   8   7   6   5   4   3   2

For Joel,
my teacher, my best friend, my mentor,
my Mike Nichols to my Elaine May,
my constant source of wisdom, and the love of my lives.

And for Josh, whose sweetness and generous spirit have helped
sustain me since the day he was born. And who gave me my Eli.

Contents

Preface

No shrinks, no pharmaceuticals, no comforting friendships, no exceptional partner (like the one I have) could come close to what writing my memoir did for my broken heart. Getting my rage, my terror, and my insights onto the page; looking at my marriage through an emotional microscope; seeing my strengths, acknowledging my weaknesses; knowing what work on my Self I still had to do; realizing how I had been held hostage. This was just what the doctor ordered. Only I found out that *I* was the doctor.

My son Dan was diagnosed with diabetes at nine months old, and at twenty-two he was diagnosed with multiple sclerosis (MS). My husband and I took care of him for sixteen years. Dan was angry right up until a few months before he died.

I wrote and was shocked to find how much laughter there had been. I had forgotten the day I had stood at the foot of his bed and said, "Goodnight, O King of Kings," and how I had bowed and then said, "Goodnight, O Lord of Lords," and bowed again and how Dan, bedridden with bedsores and legs that had stopped working and hands that were tremoring, said, "Goodnight, O Fruit of Loops." If I hadn't written it all down, I would have forgotten so much of the hardest thing I have ever done.

But the biggest healing, the biggest teaching, the most surprising thing: I would not have known how exquisitely beautiful the whole trip was.

That's how I know writing your memoir is medicine.

CHAPTER I

In the Beginning ...

Everyone has a story.

I've been facilitating Writing from the Heart workshops for forty-five years, with one rule only: when someone finishes reading, *tell her what you loved.*

When you are willing to take the chance of saying *this is who I am, these are the things that shaped me, this is where I am now,* magic happens, health happens, healing happens.

Those tiny murders that made up our early lives are marinating in our hearts, our livers, and our kidneys. Getting them out of the body and onto the page is what all doctors could be prescribing.

I've heard thousands of stories over the decades. I've watched thousands of hearts open, minds get clarity, and broken parts heal.

I have witnessed wisdom emerge and regret disappear.

I've been there when a mother and daughter fell into each other's arms after they wrote secrets they had carried for far too long. I watched as a father and his son heard each other's truths for the first time without needing to be right, and I watched them leave with their sharp edges softened. I have seen sisters reconnect and couples remember what brought them together in the first place.

I know what writing does. I know what the power of getting your perspective heard looks like. I know being listened to (and without judgment) is medicine.

In this book I have taken many examples directly from my own memoir and from other pieces that I've written for NPR and publications over the decades. But mostly I wrote this book to serve you when you're ready to write your own.

A memoir can be your written escape route from a tough childhood, it can be a trip down memory lane, it can be closure and a major healing, it can be a way to preserve your family's story. But it's not an autobiography. It's not a narcissistic unfolding of every diaper change you ever had. If it works, it's not just about what happened to you. It's why what happened matters. The *why* is what makes your story universal. And why we want to read it.

Perhaps you (or your spouse or your friends or your Aunt Margaret) has said, "Who cares?" And you internalize that and repeat, *Who would want to read my memoir? I wasn't a drug addict who after nine rehabs finally got clean and opened an orphanage in Burma. I didn't kill my father in self-defense and then start up an international foundation for girls who killed their fathers. I'm just an average person who has been told by friends that they love my emails and whose English teacher said I'm a good writer and I've had an interesting life. But who else would think it was interesting?*

Valid questions with no easy answers. If you have the desire to write your story, then don't ask those questions. You can't answer them anyway.

Maybe your ego and your soul got together and agreed to do this project as cowriters. We know your ego just wants a bit of cashmere, but your soul, ahh, your soul. She came here to expand, to learn, to deepen, to take what happened and to turn it into a work of art. The root word of *discipline* is *disciple*. Why not become the disciple of your own soul?

And instead of asking, "Why bother?" listen to poet Sean Thomas Dougherty's response: "Because right now there is someone out there with a wound in the exact shape of your words."

So are you ready? All you need is something to write with, your *attention*, which increases, and your *intention*, which transforms.

So say yes. Know this is an ongoing story. One you plopped into. But it's yours. Don't worry about the ancestors. They're dead. Don't worry about the young ones. They can't read yet.

Don't worry about your readers. You tell your truth, and they will turn the page.

These are your chapters. This is your story. You get to tell it your way.

Read these hints, pointers, and tidbits. Then follow the prompt at the end of each chapter.

Now get going!

CHAPTER 2

Why Write?

I write entirely to find out what I'm thinking, what I'm looking at,
what I see and what it means — what I want and what I fear.

— JOAN DIDEON

Me too.

— NANCY ARONIE

Why in the world do you write? And why are you writing a memoir in particular? I'll tell you why I wrote mine (which, incidentally, still hasn't gotten published). My son Dan was diagnosed with diabetes at nine months old. Doctors had never dealt with such a young diabetic baby, and they were clueless. Then at twenty-two, he was diagnosed with multiple sclerosis. He died at age thirty-eight. During the sixteen years we took care of him, the book I wanted and needed had not yet been written.

I also wrote my memoir to get ahold of how, by indulging my son, by changing the rules to make life "easier" for him, by reinforcing the message that he was handicapped in *every* way, I was actually crippling him more than the disease was. Writing about my experiences with this sick kid gave me exactly what I needed to see what I was doing. It didn't happen overnight. It was a long trip from brutal awareness to actual change.

In 1977, when Dan was six, I read *Be Here Now*, Ram Dass's landmark hippie book, and my life jumped the traditional tracks. I started driving around listening to his tapes, buying all his books, reading and underlining like a person possessed. I *was* a person possessed. I started going to silent retreats and meditating. I felt my heart opening and my mind wrestling with old paradigms, questioning everything and rejecting nothing.

In retrospect, it was almost as if I had been in training for the tsunami that was coming. Just in time, I had found my teacher.

Ram said things like, "It's all just phenomena happening and it's all unfolding perfectly," and, "There is no good. There is no bad. There just is. It's the judging and the labeling that creates the suffering."

As difficult as my boy's journey was for all of us, for the first time I had a spiritual understanding. This is not to say that the situation wasn't incredibly painful. But the pain at least had meaning. I realized that nothing about my life was random. It was about growing my soul. Who knew there was such a thing as growing your soul? Life had nothing to do with destiny. It had everything to do with how I chose to react to the constantly changing circumstances. It had everything to do with learning to let go of my need to control and learning how to be with what is. And that practice, being with what is, made all the difference in the world.

I knew my husband and I had done this thing differently from many people, and I wanted to write it, at first just to get it on the page. And then to try to understand, with a little distance, what it was we had actually done.

People kept telling us we were courageous and that we were heroes. That sounded nice, but it had nothing to do with what we were doing. The fact is, we weren't *doing* anything. We were being. We were just putting one foot in front of the other.

Later, once I saw what I had written, I realized that here was the book I had wanted. I had wanted to know that suffering doesn't kill you. I had wanted to know that there would be moments of such profound beauty I almost wouldn't have traded them for ease. I had wanted to know that this was bigger than mother and son and sickness, and I had wanted to know that I had every right to have a broken heart — and that you don't die of a broken heart. I had wanted to know that when I was stuck in the role of mother of a sick child, it gave Dan no other option than to be in his role of the sick child.

But mostly I had wanted to know that this was my soul's graduate degree, and I was going to get straight A's.

Writing it down was cathartic. Writing it down invited me to stand in a different place, and writing it down helped me begin to heal.

Writing it down showed me that fighting any of it, pushing any of it away, would have taken all the energy I needed to stay fully present. Writing it down made me realize that I could take what happens to me and turn it into something else, something beautiful, something full of grace. But in writing it, I knew that before it turned into grace I had to feel the grief. I couldn't skip the pain part.

Here are a few questions for you:

Why are you writing your memoir?

Are you writing it to get it out of your body and onto the page? If no one ever sees it, will you still be fine? Are you writing to heal?

And/or:

Are you writing to help others — and because it will be so much fun to pick out your outfit for your book signing? Because your father will finally realize how great you are, and David Weinstein will finally realize what a mistake he made by dumping you? Because now you are a bestselling author and your interview with Terry Gross has been aired three times already?

And/or:

Is it a way to tell your kids and your grandkids who you were? And because it's just powerful to write?

The question I asked myself was, *How was it possible that we were able to laugh and cry within seconds of each other?* Writing my memoir answered all my questions, including this one.

Prompt

Write your book jacket.

Go to your library (which can be your own books on your own shelves or your public library) or a bookstore, and look at a few books. Read the book jackets. Now pretend you are the editor of your book, and write your own book jacket. This will help you narrow the playing field of the thousands of things you think you should write. You don't have to stick with what you get down. But it will get you started. Beginnings are always hard. Instead of being overwhelmed by a whole blank page worth of possibilities and trying to squeeze your life into a little funnel, now you have a container.

Here's mine, just to help you get started:

In 1977 Aronie reads the landmark book *Be Here Now*. An unhappy suburban housewife, she finds a teacher and experiments with marijuana. She embarks on a spiritual journey that gives her the tools she will need for the tsunami of her son's illnesses (diabetes at nine months, MS at twenty-two, and death at thirty-eight).

The things she tells participants in her renowned writing workshops, "Write the sorrow out of your body or the sorrow will find its way into you" and "You cannot skip the pain part," become the very things Aronie needs to learn for herself.

When a dear friend tells her, "Your pain is so great Dan doesn't have room for his own," the author learns that in the middle of suffering you have to take a sharp right turn and go somewhere else.

A control freak by nature, Aronie learns to stop judging things as bad or good and begins the practice of seeing things exactly as they are, not how she wishes they could be.

In the sixteen years of taking care of their boy, Aronie and her husband begin to find beauty in the midst of horror, and together all three of them surrender as this unconventional marriage not only survives but thrives.

Thich Nhat Hanh says, "At the same time a bomb drops, a road is open."

CHAPTER 3

Uncertainty

The Roman historian Tacitus said, "The desire for safety stands against every great and noble enterprise."

Your memoir is a great and noble enterprise, but there is no guarantee that your dream of its landing on its feet will be realized. But are you a risk taker or aren't you? What do you have to lose by writing it?

In his book *A New Earth*, Eckhart Tolle says, "When you become comfortable with uncertainty, infinite possibilities open up in your life." Uncertainty is where the magic happens. "If uncertainty is unacceptable to you, it turns into fear. If it is perfectly acceptable, it turns into increased aliveness, alertness, and creativity."

Creativity is not what you have. Creativity is what you *are*. You have no choice. The only choice to make is between crippling fear and infinite possibility.

Prompt

Make a list of choices you're facing right now. Cross out the ones that are based in fear. For example: Should I quit my job and devote my time to my music with no guarantee of an income, or should I keep my security and build up my pension?

CHAPTER 4

You Don't Have to Start
at the Beginning of Your Life

Chronology is not important. *First I was born. Then my mother … then my father … then I was in kindergarten and then my brother was born and then all hell broke loose. Let me tell you all about my hell.*

This is now the reader's hell.

There are many beginnings you may be tempted to use as openers. Choosing the right one is essential. It has to be a grabber. Even though you know you don't always have to start chronologically, it's still hard to decide what will engage the reader. Here are a few of my rejects:

Reject number 1

"I'm done."

That's the way Dan greets me, and he's said it before, but this time he clearly isn't looking for a pep talk. He is looking for me to hear him.

Reject number 2

We have been catheterizing Dan for a few years, and we try to be as antiseptic as possible, but with so many people in Dan's supporting cast, the inevitable happens. He gets a urinary tract infection that goes to his aortic valve, and he ends up needing open-heart surgery.

REJECT NUMBER 3

Time does not heal all wounds, and it has been seven years since Dan left Bard, five years since he first got into the wheelchair, and three years since he's basically been living full-time on Martha's Vineyard with us.

I didn't start with any of those opening lines because I knew I had to introduce the reader to Dan in a much subtler way. So his story is tucked into this bigger story. Later in the memoir I'll probably use all three of those rejects. So it wasn't the writing that was the problem. It was the placement. Too much too soon. Here's the beginning I ultimately chose.

Rent-a-Mouth

I'm fifty-nine and coming off Half Dome mountain in Yosemite National Park. I have hiked to its peak at 8,839 feet under the guidance of twelve young women who take groups of California sixth graders into the woods and give them basic survival skills. I am here because one of their own did not survive.

Joie was murdered and beheaded. Some of these twenty-something, fresh-faced, outdoorsy girls found their friend's body in the stream where they swim and her head in the barn where they practice yoga.

I am a writing teacher and have been asked to come and do my Writing from the Heart workshop. We will swim in that stream and do yoga in that barn, and those girls will get their rage out onto the page, along with their fears and anxieties. They'll have a chance to write their own stories. And I'll get away from my son Dan, who has just been diagnosed with multiple sclerosis. I will get the chance to sort out my own story and deal with the rogue wave I have just been hit with.

I am not a hiker. I am not an athlete. When I learned we would spend five days at base camp and then go into the backcountry (I had no idea what the backcountry was) for seven, I worried that I would be expected to join the trek. I am too old to start a new hobby. Knitting is more in keeping with my newly arthritic knees. But my husband said, "You gotta go," and my soul said *go*, and then even my gut said *go*. So I went out and got myself some legitimate hiking boots. Now I hear the voice of the guy at Eastern Mountain Sports as I pull them on, pristine and never-been-touched since the day of purchase. "This is your first hiking experience? You're gonna love it, but you gotta break these babies in. So walk around in them twenty minutes a day for the month before you go." Why didn't I listen? Why didn't I at least rehearse the hiking part of the trip? Why did I say yes to sleeping on the ground without a pillow-top, to trail mix instead of eggs Benedict, to listening to the pain of twelve traumatized young women while abandoning the pain of my own traumatized boy?

Before I left, my friend Gerry gave me a mantra to repeat as I climbed, if I climbed. I thought he was going to say something like, "May all beings be happy, may all beings be happy," but instead he said, "Under your breath, with every step you take, whisper, 'Yo, Semite! Yo, Semite!'" That cracked me up, but I was afraid God would be annoyed so I added, "Oy, Yo, Semite."

The night before we set out, the women build a sweat lodge for a purification ceremony. They drag saplings from the woods, prop them strategically to create a dome-like structure, then throw blankets over the top. They gather rocks and place them in the center and then pour water on top so when the fire roars the steam will fill our thirsty lungs. We strip off our clothes and go inside and sit in a circle. One by one, we throw something metaphorically into the fire, something we choose not to bring with us up the mountain.

Some surrender their terror of returning to the trails alone; some throw in their thoughts of quitting and going home. A few feel guilty because they had issues with the victim and believe she is becoming a martyr, a slain goddess. They don't know what to do with these feelings, so they throw their confusion into the flames.

Deep listening, one of the leaders says, is a part of the ritual — a way of hearing, of being fully present without needing to control or judge.

When it's my turn, I want to throw in my helplessness in the face of my son's journey. Instead, I toss in my embarrassment that I will not be able to keep up physically. I am afraid my legs and my feet won't support me, and I know for certain I won't be able to carry a heavy backpack.

Later, alone in my bunk, I question whether I will be anything but a burden. What can I do for these girls? I am not an expert. I am not a guru. I am not a shrink. I'm a writing teacher, and I don't even actually teach writing. *OK*, I think, *then I'll do what I do best.* I'll make it safe for them to write their truth. Not just about what happened, but their own stories, the stories that shaped them. I cannot take away the pain. In fact, I will do just the opposite. I will do what I do best: I will help them feel the pain.

I have been called a midwife for words. Words that have feelings, feelings that must be acknowledged. I know what denial and numbing do. They serve nothing. When you hold sorrow in, it will find its way into your cells, your liver, your heart, your intestines, your everything. This I know for sure.

The next morning, everyone begins dividing up my stuff until my pack is much lighter. They have listened and heard and not judged. I still lag, but someone always lags with me. And when I reach the summit, they are standing on top of a huge boulder, and they erupt in rousing, spontaneous applause.

That night, around a campfire and under billions of stars, we talk about loss and death and the arbitrariness of life. I tell them about my teacher, Ram Dass, who was once Richard Alpert, the psychology professor who, with the famed Timothy Leary, facilitated LSD experiments at Harvard. I tell them that his landmark book, *Be Here Now*, changed my life, and that one of the things I learned two decades ago from Ram Dass is that everything is unfolding perfectly for your particular journey, that labeling things as good or bad keeps you trapped, that there is no such thing as time, that time is humanmade, which also means there's no late and there's no early. Everything is right on time.

I repeat a Ram Dass story that has become one of my all-time favorites. He had asked his disembodied friend, Emmanuel (and who doesn't love a teacher who talks about his disembodied friend?), who spoke through a medium, why, despite all the spiritual work he was doing — meditating, fasting, being mindful — shit still happened to him. And Emmanuel said, "Ram Dass, you're at the University of Life. Take the curriculum."

"We're all students," I tell them. "And maybe there are no answers as to why terrible things happen. Maybe it's more about not calling them terrible, more about acceptance and not fighting, not pushing away feelings that are painful but embracing them as part of our unique odyssey, our particular course of study, our curriculum."

Then I say words that I have never spoken before, but when I hear them coming out of my mouth, I know they are right. I say, "We are dancers. We bow and we sway, and we move with the rhythm of the music. We can't be rigid. We are not static. We flow. Our tragedies are our tests. And one of the ways to pass these tests is to not get stuck in the tragic, not to call things tragic but to feel the horror and at the same time know there is a teaching here."

I hear myself speaking, and I can't help but remember listening to one of Ram Dass's tapes and laughing out loud when he said his response to being called a guru was, "I'm not a guru, I'm just a rent-a-mouth."

I tell them another story about a guy who takes his painting of a sunset to a man to be framed. Most of the painting is blah, gray, almost depressing. But in the right-hand corner is a brilliant swath of magenta. Two weeks later, the guy goes to pick up his painting and the framer says, "Gee, I didn't have a frame big enough, so I had to fold over...that pink thing." I can hear you gasp. The key, I have learned, is to acknowledge the gray, the sorrow, the darkness but not to fold over the pink thing. Because there is always something beautiful. There is always light. There is always ease. There's always beauty. The goal is balance. The work is to make a bigger frame for the story. The challenge is, *How do you keep your heart open when you're in hell?*

I think of how immobilized I've become since the news about Dan's MS diagnosis, and I decide I will accept my invitation to dance. I will bend like bamboo, flow like water. And no matter how hard it becomes, I will stay present. I will make my frame bigger. I will not fold over the pink thing. And if the pink thing isn't obvious, I will look for it. Because it's always there.

The campfire warms my freezing feet. And I recognize this is exactly where I am supposed to be. I am surrounded by my guides, my teachers.

We sit in a circle, silent and safe. Their faces glow red, orange, and amber. And finally, with more joy than I have felt in months, I look around and understand I am simply a conduit for someone else's wisdom, a rent-a-mouth. And that I am taking my own course of study, my own curriculum.

And this trip is just the beginning.

The hike was one of the hardest things I had ever done. But my "teachers" were doing something even harder. They were reclaiming the landscape that had turned evil on them. I have a landscape to traverse as well. I can't reclaim it because it's all new territory. But, at the very least, my pristine boots will get broken in.

Prompt

Write three different opening sentences or paragraphs for your memoir.

> *Here are a few tips to help you get started: Beginning your memoir can be ridiculously intimidating. But I bet when you*

call your best friend the morning after the worst fight you've ever had with your lover, you have no problem knowing where to start. You are articulate. You don't miss a detail. You are passionate. You know exactly how you feel. And you have no problem figuring out where to start!

No ums. No pauses. No lack of connection with the story.

So start with one of the stories on the tip of your emotional tongue, so to speak. Go radical. Write the truth, the emotional truth.

CHAPTER 5

If Your House Is Clean, You're Not Writing

I just finished scouring that little circle around the drain in the sink. Now it's shiny perfection. I stand back and admire my work. My first thought is, *All it takes is a little elbow grease.* But my second thought is the big one: *How come you had the time to clean your sink? And you did it with so much passion and energy and gusto. How come, huh? Because you weren't writing.*

Unless you've got little fairies who come in at night and make everything spotless or hire actual cleaning people, I say you have a choice here. You want this book? You want this memoir? You want to help others? Your clean sink will not heal the world. Your book might.

Prompt

What do you do instead of writing? Write about it.

CHAPTER 6

However You Begin, Make It Real

Do not tiptoe through the tulips. Tell it like it is. Or was. Your biggest problem might be that you are afraid of your readers. Trust them. They will follow you anywhere if you are emotionally honest. Besides, why are you thinking of them? Who is *them*?

After you have the first draft, then you can do the real work. Then you can see things like, *Oops, that doesn't go here. That isn't necessary. That doesn't further the story. I already wrote that six different ways.*

Below is my example of going radical. I really had to think before I submitted this one for publication. My sister and I could have sounded like real nutcases in this piece. But I knew I had to write it, and once it was written, I knew I had to submit it for my column in the *Martha's Vineyard Times*. It also crossed boundaries because in a sense it was my sister's story, but inextricably woven into it was my story. So who gets to tell it? We both do.

Sisters

Last week my sister said, "I'm going to die in twenty-one days." If someone tells you they will be dying in three weeks, they're either planning their own suicide or their doctor has told them this is how much time they have left as a result of their terminal illness. My sister is not planning her suicide and does not have a terminal illness. She has breast cancer with some viable choices that could extend her life for who knows how many years but definitely more than three weeks. She has chosen not to take them.

"I'm ready for the next adventure," she tells me. But she doesn't ask if I'm ready.

Her oncologist, who is board certified with three medical degrees, is the most unconventional MD I've ever heard of. Four years ago when my sister was first diagnosed and couldn't decide whether to go the radiation-and-chemo route, he suggested she fly down to Tulum, Mexico, and meditate with the ancients. "You will come home with clarity," he said. And she did. "I would rather have quality of life, not quantity," she said. No drugs.

He put her on a strict diet of no sugar (cancer, he said, thrives on sugar), no dairy, no wheat. And after many other alternative remedies, within two years, two of the tumors had disappeared completely, and the third had shrunk considerably. With her life force renewed, she had energy for her ten grandchildren, her many friends, and her painting.

She published a book, went on a book-signing tour, did readings, and kept her job as a successful nondenominational minister.

Last year, when she turned eighty-four, the tumor that hadn't quite disappeared began growing again. She was experiencing severe pain, and her doctor asked her what she wanted to do this time. She said, "I think I want to eat whatever I want and have as much joy with the time I have left." Family members and friends had lists of ideas and doctors and protocols, arguments about why she should stay with us as long as there was a possibility of her survival.

Her response was, "I'm done with this part of my journey. I've had an amazing life. My kids are all settled. My grandkids have been launched. I have no outstanding issues, no unresolved story lines, no unfinished business. I feel complete and at peace."

I kept quiet.

Because her argument was hard to argue with.

My sister and I FaceTime almost every day, and it has been fun watching her savor her beloved croissant with gobs of the forbidden cream cheese, listening to her describe the delicious soup she made that morning and read me a poem she wrote years ago that she just found in her files. She calls me late at night animated about a film she just finished watching. "You have to watch it," she says. "It's on Netflix."

Is this the profile of a person who's going to die in three weeks?

"How are you doing?" my husband asks me. How am I doing? It's the question I keep asking myself. If my sister were lying in bed, weak and weeping, I'd be getting on a plane, sobbing in public, and jumping into bed with her. But she's as alive as anyone.

I'm reading a book by Deepak Chopra, a pioneer of integrative medicine. In *Metahuman* he says we go way beyond our physical selves, that our bodies are an information construct, that we don't stop at the barrier of our skin. He writes that we have no boundary, that we are constantly emitting heat and a mild electrical charge that is part of universal fields that extend into infinity. So wait. Does this mean if she dies she actually does continue on?

I have believed in reincarnation for forty-five years, since I first began reading and listening to Eastern spiritual teachers.

So of course if she dies she continues on. But I was OK with reincarnation in theory. Am I OK with it in practice?

Eckhart Tolle, another great teacher, says death is just going from form to formless. That has been at the core of my understanding of death. Can I compartmentalize and believe one thing but not want my sister to go from form to formless?

I just found out the Hebrew word for *test* has the word *miracle* right there embedded in it. (נסה, pronounced "nah-sah," has as its root the word for *miracle*...נס, pronounced "nais.")

So am I being tested? And is the miracle that I am taking my curriculum and that I will pass with flying colors?

I have always written to find out what I am feeling and thinking. And this time is no different. There's a part of me that can't stop crying and another part in awe at her lack of fear. She's always been my mentor, and now once again she's forcing me to put my money where my heart is.

Yesterday she said she was in a lot of pain but didn't want to take the morphine the doc gave her. I asked her why in the world not. And in all seriousness she said, "It's addicting." There was a pause and then we both cracked up laughing.

So now I wonder if you're thinking, "Wow, those Slonim sisters are a pair."

Well, actually, yes, we are.

One of us still in form and the other…

She died December 2, 2020, so formless.

Writing that piece made me realize I was not as cool as I thought I was. I did not want her to leave me, and I was sad that I had thought I could surrender about such a huge thing. It was only by writing it that I was able to get in touch with what I really felt.

This is proof that when you write what your subconscious or even your conscious mind is thinking, once it's on the page you can actually own it. It's not hidden underneath layers of… *I think we're running out of Thai coconut milk.*

Prompt

Write about a time you felt one way and acted another.

CHAPTER 7

Sometimes You Have to Be Shaken, Not Stirred

I learned early on, as a teenager, how to look as if nothing bothered me. I also learned to believe that I was always to blame.

On Easter Sunday, 1957, I babysat for the Lancaster family on Mountain Road in West Hartford, the fancy town we had just moved to. Mrs. Lancaster told me to take the roast out of the oven at eleven o'clock, to uncover the ham, to remove the tinfoil from the noodle casserole, and to move the cupcakes that were cooling on the baking rack into the pantry.

She didn't say I shouldn't try one of the chocolate chip cookies, or scrape a bit of the coconut frosting from the bottom of the cake plate, or slice one tiny square of fat off the ham with the pineapple ring and the cherry. And somehow I knew while they were in church praying to Jesus, the son of God, who my people had allegedly murdered, and I was at their house eating pork and sugar, that I would be appropriately punished.

When I got home, my father was trying to start the lawn mower. He pulled once. He pulled twice. And when he bent over, I thought he was checking whether it was out of gas. I playfully pushed him on the shoulder and said, "Get your hammer." My father had no hammer. He had no screwdriver. He had no measuring tape or pliers. In our house when things broke, they stayed broken. And when he would yell, "Girls, get my hammer," my sister and I knew it was a joke. This time, however, there was no joke. My father fell to the ground. His eyes were open. He was dead at fifty. I was fifteen.

For years, I was sure I killed him because I had stolen from the Lancasters' holiday dinner.

My Eastern European grandparents moved in with my mother and me the night my father died. They were small people with big hearts and even bigger fears. My grandmother's brother sported a tattooed blue number on his arm. We got no answers when we asked.

My gram was a short, square, loving woman who spoke Yiddish and broken English and walked around the house muttering "Oy." Oy, for the Nazis she was sure were hiding in the backyard. Oy, for the high price of peaches. Oy, for the pain in her fingers. "I have no strength," she muttered as she braided the dough for our Friday-night challah.

If she lacked physical strength, her spirit was a tower. When she laughed, which she did often, she ended up crying. It's a family trait. We should have bought stock in Kleenex.

My grandfather, the owner of a tiny toy store in a poor neighborhood, was also loving. He had a twinkle in his sky-blue eyes, and all his stories ended in Yiddish to protect the *yingele*, us kids. He also uttered *oy* all the time. Oy, the train was late so he had to wait on the track for an hour. Oy, the toy business is bad and maybe he has too much inventory. Oy, the *gleyzele tee* (glass of tea) is too hot.

I ingested all the *oy*s. And although my parents tried to assimilate, my roots are firmly planted in foreign soil. I took all their fears, stuffed them into my teenage being, and acted like everything was fine. There were no Nazis, you could buy fruit on sale, a toy store never had too much inventory. And I could make a joke out of anything. Even *oy*.

I was shaken by my father's death. But I was stirred by all those *oy*s.

Prompt

Write about a time when you were shaken, not stirred. Being stirred is gentle. Being shaken is shocking.

CHAPTER 8

Soul Work

Sometimes you have to leave your comfort zone to let the journey begin — you have to do the soul work.

When I got the phone call from Dan's doctor with the devastating news of the MS diagnosis, I was in the middle of reading a book called *Anatomy of the Spirit*. In it, Caroline Myss, a mystic and "medical intuitive," writes about something she calls the "sacred contract." She says we come into each lifetime with a set of lessons that our soul needs to learn. And we choose teachers who will help us manifest those lessons.

I had no trouble with the idea of a medical intuitive; in fact, I liked the possibility of such a thing. It was the word *soul* I had trouble with.

Growing up Jewish, I only heard the word used when someone had died and a grown-up said, "May his soul rest in peace." Or when my Catholic friends joked with me and said, "Oh, poor Nancy, your soul is gonna burn in hell."

When spirituality started to seep into mainstream culture and it was hip to have a statue of Kuan Yin or Buddha sitting on your coffee table next to the latest issue of *Shambhala* magazine and a well-worn copy of *The Essential Rumi*, in my typical fashion (joke first, feel later), I started making cracks about calling "1-800-the-Dalai-Lama-douche for a pure and simple soul cleanse." I also began driving around in my car listening to Carolyn Myss's tapes. Her message was no joke.

My take on the word *soul* started to shift. The more I read and the more I investigated, the more comfortable I became. At the time, I didn't know anyone I could talk to about this stuff except for my big sister. When Shirley MacLaine wrote about reincarnation in her 1983 book *Out on a Limb*, I remember calling my sis on the phone and saying, "See, we're not nuts!" But then every comic began to use out-of-body jokes in their stand-up routines. And it became our new cultural ha-ha.

I had never heard anything like what Carolyn Myss was saying, and I loved it. As I heard her words, this is what came into my mind:

Dan and I are in our cloud with our angel. And our angel turns to me and says, "So what do you want to learn in your next lifetime?" And I say, "I want to learn to let go! I have been controlling people's lives for millions of lifetimes, and I'm sick of it."

And then she turns to Dan and says, "And Dan, what do you want to learn in this next lifetime?" And Dan says, "I'd like to learn how to not be a victim. I've been a victim for thousands of lifetimes, and I'm literally exhausted from it." And our angel rubs her hands together like a magician and says, "Ooooh, have I got a lifetime for you two! One of you will come in as a baby with a nasty disease, and one of you will be the mother. The mother will be slow to 'get it,' so the child will grow up and get another disease, giving the mother a chance to evolve. I'll tell ya right now, the kid is going to have the harder trip. But they're both going to face hard work. Who wants to do what?"

Dan immediately says, "I'll be the kid." And with some relief, I am left with the role of mother. And then our angel kicks us out of the cloud, and as we tumble to Earth into our new incarnation, she yells, "Oh, and you're not going to remember any of thiiiiissss."

She basically said what Ram Dass had said. Life is just a theater piece and you are the star, and all the characters in your life just play supporting roles. All the drama is designed for your soul's growth. You are the designer, the producer, and the main character. The ego will have needs and react, but the soul will be grateful and grow.

The minute I listened to her words in that car ride, I saw Dan and me in that cloud. I felt a flood of *OMG, of course! That's what this is.* That's why he had been so difficult as a kid. It's almost as if I remembered it. That's how real it felt.

How did I know Caroline Myss wasn't a whack job? I didn't. But more than any other way of seeing existence, the sacred contract made the most sense to me. It just felt right in my gut. Which is where I know most things. I don't always trust my brain. But I have always trusted my gut.

My relationship to the future Dan and his story, our story, would not be an accident of fate or the luck of the draw or the work of the devil but rather our soul work.

For Dan, it would be letting go of his role of victim.

For me it would require a rewiring of everything I thought was important. Owning a Porsche stopped being a fantasy. Going to Carly's for brunch wasn't going to be the pinnacle anymore. Choosing *hard* with purpose was. It would require more pain than I had ever imagined, more suffering, more sacrifice. It would break us and reshape us. It would redefine love. The part I didn't know was that it would take sixteen years.

Prompt

Write a story in which you are forced to leave your comfort zone.
Do you have a sacred contract with someone? Write it.

CHAPTER 9

Write about Someone You Think Is Different from You … but Maybe Isn't

You just read about my somewhat nontraditional views on things. Let it be said that Joel, my husband of fifty-plus years, has never called me crazy, but the last thing on his mind is angels and other lifetimes.

We met on a blind date on July 4, 1965. From the beginning, I saw how different we were. But the best thing I inherited — my Gramma's intuition — told me this was the guy.

He was a nuclear engineer at Pratt & Whitney in East Hartford. I was back home from my first job out of college, teaching high school English, living at my grandparents' house in Hartford. Joel arrived in his '61 white Chevy Impala convertible with the top down. With that car, he didn't have to be as gorgeous as he was. Not that I'm a lightweight with no values, but the car alone, the summer night, the red leather seats. Come on.

He had beautiful high cheekbones, hazel eyes that changed color with the light, a graceful neck, long thin fingers, and olive skin. He was six foot two. And the bonus: he didn't know he was gorgeous. The bonus bonus: he was funny, and funny for me is the tops, the Colosseum and the Louvre Museum all rolled into one.

After dating for seven months and meeting the whole extended Aronie clan — twenty total, including his three precious brothers — I told my mother, "I want to marry Joel. I want to get into this family. They play music in the house, no one argues, the boys don't compete with each other, they laugh, they talk over each other. The father is a history buff; he lectures, they listen. They adore the mother. The food is horrible, and they all think she's a gourmet chef. None of them care about money. They worry about poor people."

My father would have loved them. He would have commiserated with Joel's dad over Adlai Stevenson's defeat. Joel's fix-it skills would have flabbergasted my father, a man with no hammer and no inclination for repairs. Joel knew plumbing. He knew electrical. And he started to know me. Everyone in my family fell in love with him. When he would pick me up for our date, my grandmother would say, "Joelila dahlink, I baked you a honey cake mit almonds on da top." She would lead him into the kitchen. There, on the little white Formica table with the Friday-night candles aglow, would be her warm offering. She'd say, "Sumpin' is wronk vit da disposal. You'll take a look?" Joel would go back to his car, bring in his toolbox (OMG, the sexiest thing, a toolbox!), get down on the floor, and spend forty-five minutes under my grandmother's sink. By the time he'd crawl out, the disposal would be purring, and my gram in her Yiddish accent would say: "I hef two voids for dat boy: vunduh ful."

One night, when we went to see *Fiddler on the Roof*, I studied his face in the darkened theater. So intent, so engaged, laughing at the same moments I was. Laughter was our native tongue. And we spoke the same dialect, fluently. Driving home, we sang "Matchmaker, Matchmaker" at the top of our lungs, and I realized we were actually more alike than we ever would be different.

One day, after almost a year spent together, I said, "We should get married, doncha think?" He showed me an article in *Scientific American* on antimatter.

I said, "We're twenty-five. That's a good marrying age, doncha think?"

He gave me a lecture on the water molecule.

I pointed out a car with the words *just married* spray-painted on the back window and tin cans tied to the back bumper.

He said, "Now the happy couple is going to fly to Hawaii for their honeymoon, wasting more of our precious oil reserves."

I said, "How many kids do you want?"

He asked me if I appreciated the beauty of a spring. Not spring the season, but a metal coil.

OK, so maybe this guy's too different for me.

But finally, he said, "Let's do it. Let's get married."

Once we got engaged, of course I brought him into our local jeweler's to buy me what I truly believed was the symbol of enduring love.

It was 1966 and this is what he said:

"I'm not buying into the De Beers conspiracy, Nance."

And this is what I said: "The who, what?"

"They're blood diamonds, Nance. People kill over these stupid things."

Then I made the mistake of saying I wanted to fly to Jamaica for our honeymoon. "The thing you have to know about flying, Nance, is that on that little flight the plane puts sixty-two thousand pounds of CO_2 into the atmosphere. And it stays there for a hundred years."

Global warming wasn't even a phrase yet. Who talks about pounds of CO_2?!

I said, "The sand is white, like in the photographs."

He said, "Flying should be limited to urgent trips."

I said (maybe under my breath), "A honeymoon *is* urgent." (And because his heart was bigger than his ideology, we did go to Jamaica.)

We got married in 1967. We were both twenty-six. I got my traditional wedding, with tuxes and bridesmaids and a wedding combo and hot hors d'oeuvres and a receiving line and everything I was programmed to want.

We moved into a duplex apartment in East Hartford, a blue-collar neighborhood near Joel's job. Mine was teaching freshman English at a high school just fifteen minutes away.

Finally, I could begin living happily ever after. And he could carry on being the only person in the world worrying about the planet and mesmerized by helical metal coils because they are so deliciously versatile.

Joel is also the funniest, kindest, easiest, most generous fellow around.

(Today he would buy me that diamond, and today I wouldn't want it.)

Prompt

Write about someone you thought you could never get along with — until you discovered your mutual native tongue.

CHAPTER 10

Turning Points and Pressure

As you build your story, set up who you were, awareness-wise, so that when we see you wake up we know how much work it took and how gradual and subtle change can be.

Until I went to my first ten-day silent meditation retreat, I had no idea what it was like to be alone and quiet for one hour, much less ten days. This experience was yet another life changer.

Here is an excerpt from my memoir:

In the middle of crying at the stoplight on Fern Street and North Main, rushing to get my older son Josh to Suzuki violin, late for picking up my mother for her doctor's appointment, worrying about Dan, and holding on to the loose wire of our '71 Mazda that Joel says will keep the car from stalling, I decide that I will definitely call that woman who owns the little Indian restaurant and looks like she is in a lovely trance all the time, in between making the best mutter paneer in the state of Connecticut and making the sweetest gulab jamun. I'm sure she knows where I can learn to meditate.

And so the Hindi woman gives me the name of a place in Massachusetts, and I call, and it's only $13 a day. Bring your own bedding and leave your larynx at home. Joel, who supports everything I do, says, "Go, babe. I'll take the kids. You go and try to be quiet. I'll do the orthodontist/orthopedic/ophthalmologist appointments." This is 1977. Most fathers I know do nothing but bring sperm to the table. So this is above and beyond the call of duty.

I sign up for a ten-day silent retreat. I still look as if I have things under control, but my life is unraveling. My neighbor's little boy shows up with vegetables from his mother's garden, and a week later I find the zucchini in the linen closet. I start making drawings late at night with all my magic markers, designing weavings I would weave if I knew how to weave. I put a potato in the microwave, turn it up all the way, and leave the house. I come home to find that the door of the microwave has sucked itself in and a sheath of plastic has melted and there is potato scattered all over the kitchen. Joel and my mother both know I need to go to this place to gain some balance. It will be an investment in their own futures. They agree to team up and take care of the kids.

It is March the first time I drive up to Barre, Massachusetts, map spread out on the passenger seat. My excitement at having left home, my worry that ten days without the kids will be so delicious I might never return, and at the same time, my anxiety about missing them to the point of running screaming (silently of course) to my car and back to my nest are bubbling up like a slow volcano, like thick bitter molasses ruining all the flavors of a good hearty root vegetable winter soup. Mmm, butternut squash, sweet potatoes, yellow Yukon golds, turnips, parsnips, carrots, and … tar.

How am I going to do this? I have not been away from my children for more than a weekend, and only if and when my sweet mother took them. Even then, I call every four hours to see if Dan is still alive.

It is damp and cold and gray, and there are sleeping bags in the hallway and cars pulling up to the entrance. And whispers. No one speaks in a full voice. There are signs that say Retreat in Process. I am given a room number, directions to an outbuilding, a schedule, and a job. I carry my bulging bags up three flights to my cell of a room. A narrow bed, a teeny sink, and a teenier mirror are the only things visible. Oh, and a few wire hangers. The bed has two moth-eaten army-issue wool blankets, and the notice taped over the sink says Please Do Not Use Hot Water and Do Not Let Water Run Unnecessarily. The same note is in the shower room way, way, way down the hall. That doesn't bother me a bit, since I have no intention of ever showering in this place. Too dark, too cold, and it's a silent retreat. Is anyone gonna come up to me and say, "Your hair needs a good washing, I have some dry shampoo"? And what do they mean no hot water? My husband would have no trouble here. He thinks people shower too often, use too much hot water, and he always turns the flow down to a trickle and thinks he's under a torrential waterfall. He's the one who should be here.

My yogini job is to vacuum the third floor. They provide an ancient Hoover. I don't mind the vacuuming. It's just that it's still dark while I'm doing it. I've gone to sleep at 4:00 a.m., but it was never a time for waking up.

Here's how it works:

I'm cozy in my cot with my threadbare olive-green twin throw (no cashmere, no fringe) and all the sweaters I own. Someone comes clumping and clanging an off-key singing bowl down the hall into my dreams. I swing out of bed onto an icy floor.

I wend my way down the long hall to the ladies'. I pee, I dress, I walk down the two flights of stairs along with all the other Zen zombies. I cross a small path outside, feel the freezing March air (Joel would call it "bracing"), and wonder what I could possibly have been thinking that brought me to this way-too-early morning misery. Then I enter the back of the dining room, and the exotic smells of cardamom and clove and cinnamon and the people hushed and lining up getting their tea become deliciously comforting. The silence is a surprising relief.

They have told us not to make eye contact. Not connecting is shockingly liberating.

I choose my mug from a vast array of pottery possibilities. I take a yellow one. I will create my own sun if none rises here in Barre. There are little labels in front of the three enormous pots of steaming liquid. Darjeeling, Bengal Spice, and black with oil of bergamot. Oh goodie, that's just what I was craving — a little oil of bergamot to start my day.

The smell is deceiving. The tea should taste like lamb korma, it should swallow like a mango lassi, it should satisfy like chicken tandoori.

Instead it tastes like my mother's Evening in Paris perfume. But the mug is warm, and that's what I need right now. Warmth and something to hold on to. The chime goes off, and I learn that after the next chime we will be filing into the meditation hall, shoes off, stomachs empty, and eyelids at half-mast.

The meditation hall is about a football field long by maybe thirty feet wide. There are burgundy velvet curtains covering the almost floor-to-ceiling windows. There are wall-to-wall mats. There are three aisles. We are instructed to go to the back of the room, if we haven't brought our own zafu (meditation pillow), and pick a pillow and pull as many blankets as we desire. Except I don't think they use the word *desire*. In Buddhism *desire* is verboten. In fact, the one hundred and twenty people gathered in this huge hall have all come to squelch desire. Bad desire. Naughty desire. Go away, desire. Come on, emptiness. Come on, equanimity. Come through, high consciousness.

Again, I am questioning why I am here. Again, I am answering: I am here because I know my life is too chaotic. I am here to quiet the constant fear that I pretend doesn't consume me every time I hear a siren when I am not with Dan. I can see the red lights flashing. They're on their way to my house. They are pulling into my driveway. They are taking my baby to the morgue. I am here because in my gut I have always known that letting the doctor induce labor so he could play golf and I could have my hair done was insane. I am here because I know somewhere deep inside that there is a hunger, a hole that a Jenn-Air self-cleaning oven cannot fill. I am here because on some level I know I have been running, but I have never had the courage to find out from what.

I like it that the hall is dark, and I feel as if I could just nap. Maybe I could learn to sleep sitting up. There are lots of last-minute small movements. People adjusting their blankets and their legs, cracking their necks. When the little bell rings there are a few more last-minute fidgetings, and then it becomes very still. Since I thought this was going to be Beginning Meditation where someone comes out and says, "OK, class. First you bend your right leg into a V, next you...," I copy what I have seen: dropping my head forward and stretching it backward, stretching out my legs, trying to reach my knees with my head. But then once it is clear that there will be no guidance, I simply do not have a clue. I sit very still for about thirty-seven seconds, then my hip begins to ache. So I move very subtly and try to find a more comfortable position without disturbing anyone. Whew. This is better. Then I sit still for about forty-six seconds more until my foot starts to feel weird. So I change its orientation very quietly and then return to stillness. After about thirty more seconds, I shift my weight onto my left butt cheek, thinking this will relieve the numbness that has begun to preoccupy me. That works for about fifteen seconds. Then I open my eyes.

Everyone is gone. Their bodies are still here but they are gone. In their places are frozen avatars, look-alike statues. They are barely breathing. Nothing is moving. I am embarrassed because I am the only one in this great hall who doesn't know how to meditate. I don't move my head, but I look as far right and as far left as my eyeballs can go. It's all the same. Very serious meditators. And I am an impostor hoping not to breathe too loudly. And then I realize no one will know I am not doing it right because they are not looking at me, since they are not here. I spend the rest of the fifty minutes squirming quietly, trying to figure out how I got into the advanced class.

I must have read the thing wrong or missed the fine print where it said this class is the real deal. These people came out of the womb in lotus position.

Finally, the bell rings and everyone seems to return to this planet slowly as they begin to stretch their limbs. Some people stay meditating. These are the real devotees. The ones who don't even know the bell rang. I am probably the only one in the room who spent the whole time praying the torture would end. I copy the stretchers. I move my neck around, I drop my head to my knees as far as it will drop, and I massage my hips. OK, now for a hearty breakfast of bacon and eggs and some home fries, maybe a few waffles with real maple syrup. And then how about a hot tub for my sore behind. Only there is no hearty breakfast. And I know this. There are some tofu clumps. Turmeric is making it yellow, so if you have more of an imagination than I, you might imagine you were eating scrambled eggs. I love food, and I can't conjure up anything mildly related to this orangey-yellow rubbery substance on my plate. There is miso soup, of course, but I have never had miso soup before and it just looks and smells like more bad tea.

We eat in silence and I am grateful for that. Otherwise I would be yelling, "This is disgusting! Anyone want to take a drive? I think I saw an IHOP nearby." I am so grateful for the no–eye contact thing. I don't want to relate. The only thing is the guy sitting directly across from me is wearing a T-shirt bearing a huge face with its mouth open in a scream. It's a little disconcerting. Where should I put my eyes? I guess on my sprouts, which I realize for the first time, having never really spent that much time focusing on the design of the alfalfa sprout, just how much it looks like sperm. Teeny tiny green spermatozoa.

Every night there is a dharma talk. A fellow named Jack Kornfield is on the "stage" with another fellow named Joseph Goldstein. I make note that they are both *lantzmen*, members of my tribe. I wonder if they too have become disenchanted with Judaism, with learning Hebrew by rote, with never feeling awe or inspiration in temples. And now here are two BuJews talking about stuff I have never heard of before.

Jack tells a story of a monk who came upon a statue of the Buddha that had dried out and cracked. The monk took his flashlight and peered in, and what he saw was a flash of brilliant gold. It turned out that inside this plain old statue was one of the largest and most luminous images of Buddha ever created in Southeast Asia. They realized that this shining work of art probably had been covered in plaster to protect it from enemies. Jack tells us that we do the same thing, that we cover over our innate nobility and shining brilliance, that just as the monks had forgotten about the golden Buddha inside that drab clay, we too have forgotten what's inside us: our essential nature. He says that much of the time we act from a protective layer, a way to defend against any hurt that might feel aimed at us.

I don't know what I've been searching for. I have never taken the time to find out that I've even been searching. Until I found Ram Dass. Clearly he is the catalyst for my being here. I know I am receiving a huge gift from Joel and my mom in having the time and silence to process this wisdom. Maybe I have come to access my essential nature.

When the ten days are up I know reentry is going to be difficult. I have gotten used to not talking. I have gotten used to no eye contact. I have begun to look forward to hot tea in the early mornings. My mind has begun to slow down, and I have begun to appreciate the little signs in the bathroom about conserving water. I wonder if I'm turning into Joel. I'm definitely not ready for driving a carpool and frying Mrs. Paul's fish sticks. I'm not even ready to use my voice.

When I get home I begin divesting. I lecture the family; I tell them we have too much stuff, that all we need are four bowls and four sets of chopsticks. Then I announce that we are throwing the TV out. Then I start cooking brown rice for breakfast, lunch, and dinner.

I move slowly, speak softly, and rise at dawn. In the past, the kids leaped into our bed as soon as they get up; now they find me sitting cross-legged on a pillow, eyes cast downward, hands turned upward, resting on my thighs. Poor nine-year-old Josh. He writes an essay for class entitled "What a Guru Told My Mother." He is sure I am about to leave home. I'm not so sure he's wrong.

That slow and conscious lifting, holding, placing, walking meditation fades into sepia pretty quickly. My new reality, the substitute for the quiet, the peace, the stillness, is my daily visit to Hilliard's candy store on LaSalle Road. "My aunt loves these Turkish jellies with the powdered sugar on top," I say to the guy behind the counter. "I'll take a medium-size box. She loves the rose flavor." I pay and leave and gobble the rose-flavored Turkish delights that my Aunt Esther might have loved if my Aunt Esther, who has been dead for seventeen years, ever got to taste the rose-flavored Turkish delights.

It is a socially acceptable addiction, sugar. It isn't like I am going to the liquor store and buying pints of vodka and sneaking nips out of a brown paper bag. Or is it? I am openly reaching into a nice white box with fine blue letters, and when the confections are gone, I just go back to Hilliard's and make jokes about my aunt who has no self-discipline. And the clerk will only think what a generous niece I am.

Jack and Joseph and the dharma talks stay with me, and I stay with my family, who put up with my biannual visits to Barre. Sometimes after I come home, I meditate for weeks. Sometimes I stop for months. There are times I return to Hilliard's, and there are times when sugar is the last thing I think to put into my body.

But always I try to remember to come back to my true nature, which at its core is simple goodness, with a little sucrose on the side.

Prompt

Write about a time you toyed with leaving your job, your home, a relationship.

CHAPTER II

You Cannot See the Gift
in What You Resist

There is a moment in any memoir when a major shift occurs, and this is an important part of storytelling. You wouldn't have a story to tell if this shift hadn't happened.

Here is an example from my memoir:

One snowy day I am in Boston for a workshop and due back on the island for my nightly "babysitting" of Dan. He can still do his own insulin shot at this point, but with great difficulty. He has figured out how to steady his tremoring hand by supporting it with his nontremoring hand and holding it close to his stomach at the same time. He can plunge the needle into his thigh. I always watch the night shot to be sure it goes in, but I don't have to do it for him yet.

The snow is falling in my favorite big floppy flakes, and I want to stay in the city and walk around in it. I want to call Dan and see if he will let me off the hook. I rehearse with my friend Gerry what I will say to keep him from exploding and give me "permission" not to return to the Vineyard.

"Don't make excuses. Don't use that apologetic voice," Gerry says. "Just say 'I'd like to stay in Boston. Can you manage?' Simple. No editorializing. No guilty 'I love snow. I hope you understand.' None of that I'm-so-sorry-you're-broken business. Just clear, plain talk."

We role-play until I think I have it down. I take a deep breath. Then I make the call. I am almost perfect. After I say, "Can you manage?" he says, "Yeah, I can fucking manage!" and he hangs up on me.

I stay, but I am miserable. I worry that his hand will slip and he won't get the right amount of insulin. I worry that he will be so out of it, he won't even be able to call 911. I worry about all the things I've worried about his whole life.

Gerry always says Dan holds me hostage. He is right. He totally holds me hostage. He guilt-trips me and he plays the victim, and I fall right into it, every time.

The next day I take an early ferry and go straight to Dan's house. And I do one of the first radical things to change our sick relationship. I charge through the door, and before he can bitch and moan at me, I say, "OK, we're done. We're done with this drama. Here's how our conversation last night could have gone. When I said, 'Dan, can you manage?' you could have said, 'No, Mom, I can't. Please come home.' And I would have been on that boat faster than you could say *islets of Langerhans*. Or you could have said, 'I can manage. Have fun in the snow.' The in-between guilt-tripping you did last night will never work again. It has never served us, but we've done it anyway. You know the definition of *insanity*? Doing the same thing over and over again and expecting a different result. Now we are in a new era. I've just gotten sane. You need me. If you abuse me, I will leave. I'm great company, and lots of people appreciate me. Until you do, you lose."

He is stunned. And I have a new resolve.

I drive home talking to myself and shaking.

But each day thereafter, just when Dan is about to do his *I'm going to kill myself* routine, he catches himself. And he starts to greet me with respect and even joy on some mornings. We start to have actual fun. When he is down, we talk about how hard it must be. He finally isn't railing, and I finally am listening.

I know things have turned because one day I walk into his room and say, "I've got one for ya. You can't walk. You can't hold a fork. You have two bedsores the size of golf balls. You have swallowing issues now. I just want to know," and I paused, "why you?"

He looks at me with a whole new expression and says, "Why not me?"

"Holy shit," I say. "You have just guru-ed!"

The shift just hit the fan. And the breeze is so refreshing!

Prompt

Write about a shift in your consciousness or behavior, a giving-in to a resistance, an end to a long-held worry. What was the outcome? If you can't think of one, write the one you want to have happen.

CHAPTER 12

Seasoning the Grill

Erma Bombeck, quoting someone else, said, "Children are like waffles. The first one should be used to season the grill and then thrown out."

You might write an entire book and then realize that it's not what you came here to say. It was your rehearsal. It was your first waffle. It was you seasoning the grill.

My first waffle was called *From Om to Oy*. It was a memoir scattered and fractured all over the place. I should have called it *From Om to Kentucky*. That's how many non sequiturs there were in it. But it greased the wheel. It got me into the habit of writing and letting go of the outcome. Which was a good thing, because the outcome was bad!

Prompt
Write your second waffle.

CHAPTER 13

Write the Same Thing
Several Different Ways

Sometimes you do have to write something five different ways. Because everyone is reading through their own wounds. Just as educators have to figure out how to teach kids who learn differently, you need to figure out how to write for readers who learn differently. And maybe, just maybe, you'll find that your own perspective changes as you write your different versions. Here are some examples from my experience:

1. One day Joel says, "If Dan could just meet a girl, everything would be all right." I lose it. "Oh my God!" I scream. "That is not what will make everything all right! How can you be so completely out of it?"

2. Joel thinks the solution to all of Dan's misery is a woman. It infuriates me. He's such a guy!!!

3. I am waiting for Dan's unhappiness to turn him into someone who has compassion for others. Someone other than himself. He has been so indulged by us that all he thinks about — and all that Joel validates — is, "Where is the perfect girl who will make me happy?" Ugh.

4. I know that Dan will not grow if he gets yet another woman to fall in love with him. He'll just continue to complain and be a professional victim. A new female in his life will not be the answer!

5. Maybe I'm wrong. Maybe Joel has something there. It's true Dan's mood lifts the minute estrogen enters

the room. I was hoping for his inner self to expand, but maybe his outer self needs the validation.

Prompt

Write one thought, one point, or one opinion five different ways. See if anything changes. Like you.

CHAPTER 14

Not Everyone Is a Storyteller

I had two sons. One would come into our bedroom after seeing a movie and in two sentences would tell us the highlights of the plot and the main characters. Then he would do almost an exact imitation of the dialogue, complete with accents. We would laugh and be moved to go see the movie ourselves.

The other sweet child (the visual artist) would come in and say, "I have to tell you about the movie. So, um, there was this guy and his... um... actually, it was really about a woman who... no, no there was this family. They lived in Switzerland or maybe it was Sweden and..."

We were parents. Self-esteem is your biggest worry when you're raising a human. It's a big responsibility. Do you tell your kid to keep his day job, that he will never be a writer or a creator or a filmmaker? Or do you wait until he knows this for himself? Or maybe just understand that his creativity will come in another form? We waited. We were kind parents with plenty of time on our hands. You don't have that time. You have to get to the point, and the point better be interesting.

Here's one where I beat around the bush and then the following piece in which I get straight to the point:

You might not know this. I for one never realized it, but all the things you are googling get stored in your buying history until you delete them. Once I found out (from a three-year-old) that keeping them open was possibly draining my battery, I started to delete. But yesterday as I was deleting, I began reading my headings one by one. They went from "how to dye your clothing using food" to "Merino wool/cashmere women's hoodie" to "Bush twin daughters" to "Abe Used Books."

The hoodie I ended up buying was red, and I realized I don't really look good in red. The reason I buy used books is that I get to buy gifts for people. I'm not sure if they appreciate getting a book with words underlined and with smudges and coffee stains.

The German Romantics said, "Tell me what you long for, and I'll tell you who you are." If you look at my Google list, you might think I'm many people. I have a friend with multiple personality disorder, and when she first told me about it, I thought, *Wait, don't we all have that? And why is it called a disorder?*

She said, "When I wake up in my gorgeous Fifth Avenue NYC apartment I'm a grown woman, and when I leave I ask my doorman how his kids are, but when I get to my therapist's office, I'm on her floor, sucking my thumb because I'm a year and half, and when I get into the cab to come back home, I'm swearing like a sailor at the poor cabbie." The poor woman was so split off, and I always wondered which personality I was talking to. Obviously if it had been the baby, I would have known. I think it would be so interesting to be a psychiatrist and be in the same room with people with multiple personalities. I probably would end up taking them home with me.

My list was so varied and all over the place that I asked my husband, just for laughs, for his list. His Googles went from "the Wright brothers" to "Michael Moore's *Planet of the Humans*" to the "wildly complex anatomy of a sneaker" to "carbon-neutral bioceramic dome homes."

You have to ask, How did these two people ever get together based on their interests?

That's a good question. How do any two people get together? That's one of those rhetorical questions that cannot be answered in just one short piece.

Now for the piece where I get straight to the point:

You might not know this. I for one never realized it, but all the things you are googling get stored in your buying history until you delete them. But as I was deleting, I began reading my headings one by one. They went from "how to dye your clothing using food" to "Bush twin daughters" to "Abe used books."

The German Romantics said, "Tell me what you long for, and I'll tell you who you are." If you look at my Google list, you might think I'm many people. I have a friend with multiple personality disorder, and when she first told me about it, I thought, *Wait, don't we all have that? And why is it called a disorder?*

I read an article that answered the question. It said people with this disorder keep all their different personalities separate, whereas most of us manage to integrate all our inner beings and are a healthy conglomeration of our multiple aspects.

My list was so all over the place that I asked my husband, just for laughs, for his list. His Googles went from "the Wright brothers" to "Michael Moore's *Planet of the Humans*" to the "wildly complex anatomy of a sneaker" to "carbon-neutral bioceramic dome homes."

You have to ask, How did these two people ever get together?

In about the eighth month of dating we watched a Sid Caesar TV special. We were on the floor laughing hysterically. I had found our mutual connection: our shared native language was laughter. Over more than fifty years of marriage, laughter has sustained us through thick and very thin.

The other day we bought a peony plant, and on the way home I was reading the directions. I turned to my husband and said, "It says it won't bloom for three years." There was a long pause. And then he said, "Uh-oh."

And then we laughed.

Prompt

Write two pieces, one where you beat around the bush and never get to the point and the other where you get right to the point.

CHAPTER 15

You Will Not Be in the Room

Remember, when your reader is lying comfy on the couch and it's raining and there is a fire going and she just finished a cup of hot cider she mulled herself, you will not be in the room with her. She won't know what the passage she is reading smells like unless *you* have chosen the right words. She won't know the color blue on the bedspread you're describing unless you describe it so she sees it.

Here's an excerpt from *Vera*, Carol Edgarian's historical novel about the 1906 San Francisco earthquake. You can feel in this short passage what it must have been like for the two young girls in the story. Here's Vera thinking:

> How many months it would take for the most basic parts of city life to resume — water flowing from the tap, the cable cars humming, a school day with the dread nuns. There'd be no gas or electricity or telephone service for weeks; no water, except the meager cupfuls doled out in the relief lines. It had taken less than a minute for the citizenry of San Francisco to be reduced to the hunter-gatherers of old. Cooking over fires, sleeping in coats, relieving themselves over buckets or in trenches. Society, with its rules and strictures, would have to be rebuilt brick by brick.

And here's a beautiful example of an author helping you to feel like you're right there with the characters, from one of my favorite writers, Jane Lancellotti. This is from a story in progress:

> Later, in his apartment, Ben played one of the more esoteric prizes from his record collection. My memory will

only allow that it was African American and required tremendous linguistic ability on the part of the singer who managed to be both otherworldly and inescapably human. He seemed mollified to think that it was possible to find the human point in the rise and fall of a song. I had thought that it still wasn't too late to convince him of the human point growing inside me, but sleep was dunking me under with both hands. I finally surrendered, my arm slung over Ben's chest as the far off voice of a solitary African sawing at the universe drifted upstairs.

You aren't there with your arm slung over Ben's chest, but you can feel the far-off voice, and you can feel sleep dunking you under because the word choices are perfect.

Prompt

Write a vivid description of something so we can feel — with as many senses as possible — what you're talking about.

CHAPTER 16

Insights

Take your insights seriously. You were given a flash of luminous mind. Pure clarity.

It wasn't your imagination. It was your third eye opening for a microsecond. You're not nuts. You just got a gift of divine wisdom. Don't waste it. Don't question, "Why me?" Be like my son Dan. Say, "Why not me?" Then take that insight and write it down immediately because you will forget it. It will be so profound you will talk yourself into thinking, *How could I forget such a thing?* Trust me. You will forget such a thing.

I am often asked why I write and why I encourage others to do the same. For me, it's to find out what I'm thinking, what I'm feeling, where I'm stuck. And if I'm lucky, I get a new insight that might lead to some healing.

The last prompt I gave to my online writing class was "I have a ridiculous amount of..." One woman wrote, "I have a ridiculous amount of gardening books." Another wrote, "I have a ridiculous amount of shoes." A third wrote about her massive collection of ceramic animals.

I have learned that I can't give an assignment unless I write it too. So here's a piece I wrote in which I gained an important insight:

I have a ridiculous amount of Christmas lights. They adorn the fireplace. They climb up the living room wall. They droop around the periphery of the kitchen. They twist and turn and line every surface of my little cabin. I have them outside too. There are strings of them that go from one tree to the next, lighting up the whole entrance to my yard and the full length of my driveway.

At first I bought them at the Christmas Tree Shop. Boxes of them for only a dollar a box. Then Restoration Hardware started selling them with beautiful copper wire, teeny ones that had an amber glow that I loved even more than the white ones.

So why this obsession with Christmas lights? Oh no, Nancy please don't go there. Let's not dredge up stories about your painful childhood Christmas-envy wound. How every December 25, first thing in the morning, all the kids in the neighborhood went outside yelling the spiritual mantra, *Whatcha get? Whatcha get?* And how you had to answer, "I'm Jewish." How eight tchotchkes, one a night, could never compete with an American Flyer sled or a pair of brand-new Sonja Henie figure skates. So don't go there. Just enjoy your ridiculous amount of Christmas lights and let go of it.

Actually, I have let go of it (by writing about it a hundred times). See how writing helps?

Turns out a cigar is just a cigar. I love the lights because I love the lights.

There is a bigger problem, however, and that is that I keep them on all the time.

My poor husband, whom I've dubbed the Energy Czar, has asked me in the nicest of ways why I need the lights on constantly even when we're not in the house. My answer has always been that the plants need them on. The cats need them on. The house itself needs them on.

He shows me our electric bill. Apparently we used 950 kilowatts last month. I'm almost thinking *kilowatts, schmilawats*. He says we have a washing machine and a dryer and a refrigerator and a hot water heater, and you're right, the lights aren't using up that much. But it all adds up.

The thing is, I have tried to turn them off. Really, I have. But I just can't do it.

One day recently I looked around and made myself ask, *Why do I leave the lights on?* I knew it wasn't for the plants. I knew the cats couldn't have cared less, and the house itself has never said anything like, "Thank you for the perpetual Christmas."

I stood with my coat on, making myself go deeper and dig out the real reason I would thumb my nose at saving money and honoring my husband's wishes. And so I wrote about it. And lucked out and got the insight.

I grew up in a household that worried about what people would think. Our house wasn't designed for our comfort. It was done up for company so that when they left, they would say about us, "Wow, those people have elegant taste." Or whatever my mother was hoping they would say.

So there I was, thinking that if someone came in while I wasn't home and saw all this adorable twinkle in the house they'd ... (long pause) what? Think more of me? I'm afraid I came up with yes.

With that I switched off every light. And in doing so, I made a little progress in switching off my understandable but no longer relevant need for approval.

Just as it has to be dark outside for us to see the stars, sometimes it has to be dark in my house for me to see the wisdom.

And here's one by Molli Hourihan, a writer and a mom, in response to a prompt in one of my workshops:

> I own a ridiculous amount of ... parenting books. What to eat when you're pregnant, how to get your baby to sleep, how to get your baby into a car seat. How to raise a respectful child, how to raise a Jewish child, what to do with a wild child. Parenting the oppositional child, parenting the anxious child, how parents should listen to their child. When my son was born, I devoured these books like bonbons. Jonas slept eighteen hours a day. I didn't realize how lucky I was that he took three big fat naps before dinner. I credited it to my sleep books and bragged to and secretly judged my friends in that competitive kind of listening for common pitfalls I'd read about, like nursing on demand or napping in the car seat. Except I was already being swallowed up by my own rigid standards.

When my daughter was born three years later, and barely slept until her measly afternoon nap, I knew my bubble had burst. My kids are eleven and thirteen now. I am washing dishes and listening to *Self-Compassion for Parents* through my AirPods. This book is basically about accepting yourself for not being perfect. Without thinking, I yell at my kids to clear their plates. Perfection is a fantasy. But the menu looks delicious, and I'm hungry for more.

The word *ridiculous* says it all. Bring humor and humility to one of your obsessions, and what will you get? Insight into everyday pain. The irony: my best intentions — to buy all the books and soak in perfect parenting — was that it was getting in the way of being present for my kids. Reading it, googling, downloading it, is not living it. But writing it helped me see it; that it is hard for me to close the books and trust my own instincts. Being present is advice I could read in a book, but finding out what was blocking me, I needed to write that for myself.

Because I am terrified of being a bad parent.

Prompt

Write about a life-changing insight.

CHAPTER 17

Sometimes Our Stories Begin
with a Crack

There's nothing subtle about life. It comes and goes, ebbing and flowing, but sometimes it comes crashing like the surf in a nor'easter. Your story and my story are about life, which is not always simple or smooth. Here's an excerpt from my memoir, a part of my story that grabbed me out of a sweet, peaceful place and yanked me into a reality I wasn't prepared for:

It's Sunday morning. The perfect lovemaking morning. My husband passes me a joint. I take a hit and pass it back. "The greatest thing about smoking pot as grown-ups," I say, "is we don't have to be paranoid about the parents." I pause, inhaling, and then let out a big poof: "We *are* the parents!" We crack ourselves up.

Joel and I started smoking marijuana in our thirties. We are children of the '50s, and *Reefer Madness* was our only reference to the drug. When people used it, apparently they jumped out of windows. So when a former student of mine showed up with three joints as a baby present when our first son was born, I was outraged. "Out!" I screamed. "Whatever were you thinking?!"

"Mrs. Aronie," she said, "this will change your life. I'm just going to leave them here on the mantel."

It took two months before Joel said, "Come on, let's try it."

"Absolutely not," I barked. "I'm already close to the edge. You, you can do it. You're more grounded." And so he did. And something happened to him that had not happened before. He was running his fingers through my hair. And he was looking at me. And he was whispering. And our lovemaking was slow, and I finally had time to catch up. Later, I said, "You are going to have to do this daily."

It took me a few more weeks to build up the courage, but what my student had said was true. Marijuana changed our lives. Neither of us had ever been into alcohol. My parents had a bottle of Seagram's 7 they kept in a little cabinet in the living room. Every New Year's Eve, they'd fill two shot glasses, toast each other, then return the bottle to its little home for 364 more days. Joel's father made terrible wine and drank a juice glass of it at every meal. Pot became our weekend date-night, altered-state ritual. It was $15 an ounce, and an ounce lasted us the whole year.

I fiddle with the radio, trying to find sexy music. Joel doesn't need special music. He's reaching for me, and now trying to find the "right" soundtrack for sex seems like the wrong priority, so I settle for classical.

We know each other's bodies well. We are a synchronized swimmer and an under-the-big-tent act. I am Esther Williams and he is all three Karamazov brothers, no fear and exquisite timing. The Cleveland Orchestra (or maybe it's the Boston Pops) is playing the "William Tell Overture" and we are with it, note for note. At the exact same moment that they crescendo into an electrifying climax, so do we. And then (how could we have known that they had recorded a live performance?) there is a tidal wave of applause. I jump up and, in all my naked glory, I bow to my invisible and enthusiastic audience. Thank you to the mezzanine, thank you to the box seats, thank you to the first balcony, and a sweeping bow to the cheap seats, and I collapse laughing into my husband's delicious, welcoming arms.

How did we get this lucky? Even though we live in West Hartford, Connecticut, the capital of ordinary in the so-called Land of Steady Habits, where it's against the law to be spontaneous, where I am sometimes looked at with condescending glances because I am not wearing Laura Ashley and I have the audacity to let my unruly curls rule, I am the happiest I have ever been.

It's 1990, and our older son, Josh, is twenty-one and enjoying his lacrosse scholarship in his junior year at Ripon College in Wisconsin. Dan is nineteen, in love, and at Bard College in New York, where, at the orientation, the dean looked out at the incoming freshmen class and said, "We may not have been your first choice, but you were ours." No one has ever said that to my Dan.

And while our friends are going through withdrawal with their empty-nest syndrome, we are celebrating finally being alone. And, best of all, life is free from the reign of terror in the next room, from Dan, our boy who was diagnosed at nine months old with juvenile diabetes and who has held us hostage ever since.

The phone interrupts our reverie. It's Dan, who never minces words. "Mom," he blurts, "I can't get a hard-on."

What he has said is too jolting to respond to the irony of the timing. "What's going on?" I ask.

"I just told you. I haven't been able to get a hard-on for two weeks."

"Where is Jamie?" I ask.

"Here," he says. His girlfriend gets on the phone and says, "Hi, Mrs. Aronie," and I say, "Come home, the two of you, we'll figure this out." And then I add, "Don't worry." But I am totally worried. Extremities. He's had diabetes for almost nineteen years. I have prayed that nothing like this would happen. But here it is. My prayers have not been answered.

They arrive that night and, because I am a fixer first, I say, "We'll sell the house if we have to. We will fix this." First thing Monday morning, Joel drives the kids to Yale New Haven Hospital. My doctor friend, Barbara, has gotten us an appointment with a top neurologist. It is late when they return. I am still in my home office, writing. Dan's face is dark. He throws a brochure on my desk. On the cover is an elderly couple with one word, in big block letters, *IMPOTENCE?*, with a big, fat navy-blue question mark.

"You let this fucking doctor give him a brochure with eighty-year-olds on the cover?" I scream at Joel. "With that word? He is nineteen. He's fucking nineteen!"

"Nance, Nance, calm down," says my sweet husband, whose face is a darker shade of gray than Dan's. "What could I do?"

"What could you do? You could have shot the guy."

We make another appointment, and this time I go too. The doctor says it's anxiety. It's emotional. He's a young man. It's fairly typical. We repeat for the twenty-seventh time that Dan is a juvenile diabetic and has never had trouble in the sex department. Isn't it possible that this is connected to the disease?

The doctor gives us a flat no and enrolls Dan in a sleep clinic. They put a plastic ring-like monitoring device around his penis to record how often and how long the erections last, and how firm they are. When we pick him up after one night, the doctor's diagnosis is stress. He dismisses us as if we are parents with no boundaries, interfering in our son's sex life.

Dan goes back to Bard. It's spring semester, and he is in the middle of rehearsals for *View from the Bridge* when we learn that one of our family friends — one of Dan's closest — has taken his own life. We have to drive the four hours to Annandale to tell Dan the news and bring him home for the funeral.

Afterward, he makes it through the play, and he even makes it through his freshman year. But he complains of numbness in his hands and quits before Thanksgiving his sophomore year. He wants to move to Colorado, where his first love lives, and when I protest that I'm worried about his health, he assures me the numbness is gone. He promises me if that it comes back, he'll go to the ER. He drives out to Denver, and calls from a pay phone every time he crosses a state line. With each call he assumes a different character and sings a different song.

"Hello, Mama, this is the Big Bopper speakin'. You know what I like. Chantilly lace and a purty face, a ponytail hangin' down . . ."

He sounds so happy, my stomach relaxes. I think it is good for him to be on his own, free from my hovering energy.

Within three days, he gets a job selling fire alarms door to door. He loves it because it is a lot like acting. He enjoys demonstrating the fancy apparatus. He is paid on commission and in no time is racking up some good numbers.

After a month, he calls us one night, and we can't quite

understand him. His voice is garbled, but what we finally discern is that in the middle of a sale he suddenly couldn't talk. The customer thought Dan was drunk. Humiliated and embarrassed, he left the man's house and called us. We tell him to go to the emergency room. We're flying out tonight. He insists that we not come. It is hard to decide if we are babying Dan and keeping him from his independence. So we stay home. By the phone.

A friend takes him to Denver General Hospital, where he has an MRI and a CAT scan. I get the call late the next afternoon.

I am outside. I lower myself onto a bench in the yard. The doctor on the other end of the line says, "Your son, I'm afraid, has had a stroke."

I see the buds on the trees, that chartreuse yellow-green tender color almost unfolding in slow motion and blocking the doctor's words. I take in bits but not the whole. I think I say, "Thank you. Is Dan there now? Can I talk to him?" Dan gets on the phone and sounds like he is auditioning for a lead role in a zombie film. I tell him we're on our way. The doctor calls back as I am making the reservation.

It isn't a stroke after all. The results of a spinal tap show that Dan has multiple sclerosis.

"This is a much better diagnosis," the doctor says. I have no idea what MS is. All I can picture is Jerry Lewis and kids in wheelchairs, making no distinction between MS and muscular dystrophy. I don't see how this can possibly be a better anything.

By the time we land, I have booked Dan an appointment with a neurologist. He shows us pictures of the plaque on Dan's brain. That night Joel says, "Did you see the amount of plaque? This is bad, Nance. This is very bad."

Me? I never look at the scans, and I refuse to turn on my emotional hearing aid. I do not hear *plaque*. I do not hear *bad*, I do not hear *very bad*.

This is the beginning of our very different approaches to this new curveball that has hit me square in the belly. When we get home, we go to the library and read everything we can find on MS. Multiple sclerosis is a disease of the central nervous system.

It attacks the protective sheath that covers nerve fibers and causes communication problems between the brain and the rest of the body. The cause is unknown; there is no cure. Holy shit. What happened to *everything is unfolding perfectly*?

Combing through a bunch of articles, I find a Dr. Hans Nieper in Germany, who is doing cutting-edge work with MS patients, mostly with diet. I say, "Joel, we have to go to Germany. This guy is having great results, especially if he gets the patient when he's first diagnosed." Joel says, "Nance, we're not flying to Germany to some quack who probably charges an arm and a leg." I say, "So we'll pay an arm and a leg. We have to go, Joels, we have to go. I am begging you." He says, "We're not going. We don't have an arm and a leg. We don't even have an arm. If this guy is legit, don't you think every neurologist and the whole MS community would know about him?" "No," I say, "I don't." He says, "The flight alone will cost a fortune, and then how long do we have to stay there? We can't miss work." I say, "What are you talking about? Work has no meaning right now. This is the only thing that has meaning." I don't fight hard enough. I'm not sure myself whether Dr. Nieper is a quack. So no, we don't go.

There is no WebMD. No Google. No TED Talks on MS. So I track down every healer. I buy every book, I call every expert, I evaluate every herb, and I investigate every supplement. I get every story of someone who knows someone whose cousin has MS and traveled to Kazakhstan to see a guy. And then there is this Korean doctor who has a spa in the Bavarian Alps, but you have to commit to staying for six years. And maybe if Dan went vegan and consumed no animal fats. And if he could just meditate — there is a new technique that not a lot of people have attested to but there is proof that it cures MS; it involves never inhaling another drop of oxygen. I will talk Dan into it.

Prompt

Write about a phone call that had an enormous effect on you.

CHAPTER 18

Your Story Will Take Many Turns, from Joy to Pain and Then Back to...?

We've all done it, engaged in premature sighing. There are so many moments when we heave a big sigh of relief, and two seconds later a Mack truck hits us. After we clean up the debris from the crash, we realize it was too soon to let out that sigh. Here is what I wrote in my memoir.

My Trip to Rhode Island

Dan has a crush on a hair stylist at Supercuts in Narragansett, Rhode Island. Our cousin Bert, who lives in Newport, has invited us to come see him a million times. Dan agrees when I suggest we combine the visit with a haircut.

I have been doing push-ups so I can lift the manual wheelchair onto the bike rack on our old Volvo wagon by myself. It gives me independence for my travels with Dan; I can just take off when Dan says, "Let's go."

On the ferry to the mainland, we pass the time by listing the jobs we've held. He says, "Dishwasher at the Yellow Barn in Avon." I say, "Waitress at the Stevensville Hotel in the Catskills." He says, "Sous-chef at Frank's Steak House in Hartford." I say, "Go-go dancer at the World's Fair." He says, "Nude model at Simsbury Art League." I say, "What? You were a nude model???" He says, "Yeah." I say, "Well, it happens, so was I. Does that mean we cancel that one out?" He says, "No. It double counts." We continue. I say, "Drama coach in my living room for little kids." He says, "Assistant drama coach in our living room for little kids."

And then we reminisce about that disaster. He was thirteen, and I wanted to give him some responsibility and a chance to feel good about himself. But there was one kid we both almost killed. The child repeated everything anyone said, and we couldn't stop him. When I told his mother I'd refund her money, she begged me to let him stay. It must have been her only two hours of peace.

We keep going with our job lists until I say, "For your age you've racked up a lot of work hours. Either you have been a really hard worker, or you couldn't hold down a job." We laugh, both knowing it is the latter.

Once we hit the open road, we blast WHJY 94.1 Providence on the radio. We sing at the top of our lungs: *Take it easy, take it easy, don't let the sound of your own wheels make you crazy.* The Eagles have no idea what they're doing for me this fine morning.

I ask Dan what he likes about the girl at the salon. He says, "She's smarter than me and funnier." He doesn't say anything about her looks, which makes me happy. Maybe he is growing up.

We enter Rhode Island and Dan says, "I have to go to the bathroom."

"Can you wait?" I ask. "We'll be at the salon in ten minutes."

"No! I have to go now!"

He is squirming and making sounds of desperation as I take the first left I see. It's a narrow dirt road into — a cemetery. I put the car in park, jump out, open his door, and literally pull him out. I lean him against the car. I unzip his pants and don't even hesitate. I take his penis out. And since I have not done this before, I don't take it out far enough and he pees all over his pants. And me.

When I get him back into the car, the mood has downshifted. Not only are we both embarrassed but now he can't see Tiffany.

We arrive at Bert's. He gives Dan dry clothes, but Bert is much shorter, so my six-foot-two son looks like Lurch with attitude. The trip is ruined. I can't fix this one. We sleep over, and I suggest we stop to see Tiffany on the way home.

"What would she want with a cripple like me?" he says. Vintage Dan. We return to the ferry terminal to the Vineyard with the radio silent the whole way.

Prompt

Write about a time everything seemed fine and two seconds later it fell apart.

CHAPTER 19

Pay Attention to the Coincidences

Deepak Chopra talks about something he calls "synchrodestiny," the merging of coincidence and destiny. It's a way to recognize the intelligence of the Universe. He says that if we celebrate the cosmic dance, as he calls it, trust that there is a rhythm to life, and live in harmony with that rhythm, everything we desire comes to us effortlessly.

So coincidences may seem like coincidences, but really, if you are in the present moment (good luck — I know how hard that is), then you realize they will be little miracles designed completely to support you.

Here's a piece I wrote that was aired in the '80s on NPR:

The Signs Are Everywhere: You'll See Them If You're Looking and Not Talking

I have always been a talker. My parents said that even when I was little, when they would come home late from an evening out, they would rush into my room outraged that I was still awake, only to find me sitting up in bed *talking* in my sleep. To no one.

I come from a family of talkers. We talk over each other, thinking the louder we yell, the bigger the possibility someone will listen. But since there are no listeners in this crowd, no one really hears anything.

A poet friend of mine said, "The most important trait a writer can have is listening. And you can't listen if you're talking." So I began genuinely trying to be a listener. Consciously working at it. One night my husband and I were driving down Massachusetts Avenue in Boston. I said, "I need you to help me with something.

I need you to alert me when you see me talking at a party or a dinner or even with just one friend, or with you, for that matter, like even if we're at a function or a gathering and you look across and see me moving my lips and going on and on, would you just give me a high sign, something gentle, not like screaming across the room, 'This is a good time to try that listening thing, babe.' Just a wink or a nod, something subtle so no one else knows what we're doing. I can't seem to do this myself. I just slide into talking because it's so easy for me and I'm just so used to it. It's like smoking, it's a habit."

I ranted on for probably ten miles without taking a breath. And then we came to a red light. And there on my right was a Mexican restaurant with a bright neon sign that read Grande Boca (big mouth). We laughed for five minutes straight.

Here's another example of coincidence:

I sang tenor in the Congregational church choir for three years. But when Dan was sick and getting sicker and I was feeling blue and then bluer, I quit the choir. I was taking a walk, and I remember saying to myself, "This is what depression feels like."

"I am feeling bereft," I said to no one. "I haven't had a light feeling, that connection, that high, that heart-open space. I feel closed. So God," I said, "I had all these miracles, not really miracles, but things that made me know you exist, and now, nothing. I also know this is the stupidest conversation I have ever had. If you had been in my head or overheard what I said, you'd have rolled your eyes and maybe considered offering me some medication." But I felt like I had no one else to have this conversation with. And then I thought: *I need a sign. Just a little something. To remind me.* "I was getting signs every minute for years. But it's dried up. You've given up on me. Or did I give up on you? I know it has everything to do with Dan, but if you could just do one of your little coincidence things." And then a weird thought crossed my addled brain. And I said, "You're not upset with me that I'm singing in a gentile choir, are you?" In a flash, a millisecond, as long as it takes to say you're not upset, there directly in front of me was a tree that had fallen from the recent storm into the crook of another tree ... in the shape of a *cross*! I think I gasped and looked up (because I am programmed to think God is up) and said, "Good one. All set now. I'm back." And I was.

Now that I know about synchrodestiny, I know that's what that was. Not a coincidence at all.

This listening thing is like anything difficult. It becomes a practice. My husband is a great listener (that's a good thing for me, ha ha). In a way listening is a form of love. Anne Lamott wrote, "Love is the whisper of wire drum-brushes. And while everyone has to make a living and show up for family, listening is optional: you have to make a conscious decision to begin listening harder."

Wow. I love her.

Prompt

Start looking for a synchrodestiny in your everyday life. Pay attention. Listen harder. Be in present-moment awareness. Then when you find a synchrodestiny, write it up.

CHAPTER 20

Don't Be an Expert: Be an Expert

There are things you know. Write them. There are things your subconscious knows. Trust them. There is a whole lot of stuff you don't know. Either research before you write, or don't even attempt to fake it. We'll know you're pretending to be an authority. If you can admit there's something you didn't know but learned on the spot, that gives the reader the opportunity to learn that something with you. You aren't the expert. You're the student. The reader can really relate when they aren't made to feel stupid. Your vulnerability is an invitation to the reader to become a partner.

Last night I was at a Zoom birthday party. In our introductions as we went around "the room," we were asked to identify our pronouns. It wasn't the first time I'd encountered such a request. Last year when I was training for a political fundraiser on another Zoom call, it was the first thing we were asked to do. That time I had no idea what in tarnation they were talking about. Soon after, a close friend told me she was now going to be a "they." "Huh?" I remember saying. She said, "Nance, some people don't neatly fit into the categories of male or female. Some don't identify with any gender. Some people's genders change over time. It's just respect we're asking for." I started to understand, but as we kept talking I kept making mistakes, which they kept correcting.

At first I had a lot of trouble navigating the language. My feelings were not the problem. The grammar was. How could I say "they" are coming to visit when it was one person? I asked my friend why they couldn't come up with a better word. They were able to laugh with me, and I was able to suspend any judgment.

After I hung up from the celebration last night, where we

were also asked where we lived and who the indigenous peoples were, I felt old. A fabulous kind of old. I thought about how far we've come. And look what these kids care about.

My first encounter with a gay person was in 1954, when I was in seventh grade. After school everyone went to Maxwell Drug for root beer floats and potato chips while we waited for the city bus. There was a mirror that ran the full length of the shop and stools that lined the full length of the mirror. I was standing behind a girl whose reflection I could see clearly. I must have been staring because she turned with such venom and said, "What choo lookin' at?" I couldn't say, "I was looking at you because you don't look like anyone I've ever seen before." I couldn't say, "You are a girl but you look like a boy." I couldn't say it, not because I was afraid of hurting her feelings or what she would say back. I couldn't say it because I didn't even have the language.

In my family I had heard the Yiddish word *feggilah*, which was used to describe a boy who was feminine. It was sometimes spoken in hushed tones but never in derision; it seemed like it was just a description. This situation I found my thirteen-year-old self in was brand-new.

But being taunted for being different was not new. I was tall for my age and was called Lanky Lou and Stretch, and when they really wanted to hurt me they called me dirty Jew and kike. The snowballs tossed my way had stones in them, and walking home from school was often a scary ordeal. Kids who wore glasses, anyone with a limp, kids who were chubby, kids whose parents got divorced, anyone who had anything different had to be on guard.

Time doesn't heal all wounds, but it can't help itself when it comes to paradigm shifts. And in my old age, the age I am cherishing now, I have seen a bunch of them. For one small example, how did we manage to go, in such a short time, from smoking on airplanes to being made to stand out in the cold in front of our workplace buildings to smoke? And indigenous peoples? I don't think they were in my consciousness till I was a grown-up and read Howard Zinn's *A People's History of the United States*.

Last night most of the partygoers were young. And when I hung up I thought about what I cared about when I was their age. How I hated my curly hair. How many calories a scoop of mint chip ice cream was. If the cute guy who had asked me for my geology notes would call me. It's embarrassing.

I also realized (not for the first time) that it's those young people's (did I ever think I would use the phrase *those young people?*) job to teach me to move forward. I thought I was the teacher, and I also thought I was always ready to learn. But I have been noticing I do not always like being taught.

My grandparents saw the advent of the car, the telephone, the television, women doctors, the polio vaccine, the WPA, the atomic bomb, jet planes, transistor radios, antibiotics, using *Ms.* instead of *Miss* and *Mrs.* (maybe the *they* of its time).

So if my Gram and Pappy could adapt to all those changes, certainly I can figure out a way to say "they" without wincing. Respect for my fellow human must win out over my love of Strunk and White's perfect-sounding grammar.

At least I knew and was proud to answer that the indigenous peoples of where I now live are the Wampanoag.

Unfortunately, I still think about the mint chip ice cream.

Prompt

Write a piece that incorporates something esoteric or includes information that might illuminate or instruct.

CHAPTER 21

Don't Shy Away from Taboo Topics

When Dan was still walking, I started to film him. In retrospect, it was a brilliant thing to have done. I was putting a camera between my terror and his rage. He had such a huge ego and had studied acting at Bard, so it was a natural for us to collaborate on this film. I had asked him if there was anything off-limits and he said no, film it all. The day he came home from heart surgery (because of that UTI that traveled to his aortic valve), his girlfriend, Sarah, was lifting him onto the bed and I was filming. He looked like a cadaver, sunken eyes, bone thin, in contrast to her fresh-faced glowing beauty. As she was lifting him onto the bed, she said, "Oh no! The urine bag! It's stuck in the wheelchair!" Somehow she was able to hold him up and flip the urine bag onto the bed. And I filmed it all.

Later that week I got a call from a friend who owned a gallery in Hartford, asking me to come and do a presentation onstage. I said, "Absolutely no. I'm crying all the time. My son is sick, and I won't be very entertaining. But thank you." And then suddenly I thought, *Wait, I have fifty hours of tape of Dan. What if I get someone to put twenty minutes together and bring Dan onstage with me and show it on the big screen? He'll get a standing ovation and finally know that what he is doing is not for naught. He'll possibly see himself as a teacher, showing others what it's really like to struggle and survive.* I posed the idea to Dan, and he agreed.

A young woman who had just graduated from New York University's film school had just taken my workshop. I called her and asked her if she could put together about twenty minutes of film, no need for editing or continuity. Just so I could show his story up on the big screen. She agreed, and when she gave me the beautiful twenty minutes back, she had cut the part where Sarah had said, "Oh no! The urine bag..." When I asked her why she had cut it, she said, "Well, I just figured he'd be embarrassed and people would be uncomfortable."

When I tell this story in class, I end with, "The urine bag is the story! Don't cut the urine bag!"

When You Wish the Shit Would Hit the Fan (or at Least the Porcelain)

Try Colace. MiraLAX. DulcoEase. Trulance. Stool softeners. Flaxseeds. Prunes. Dates. Roughage.

Dan stops being able to move his bowels. After we try everything in aisle three for constipation, we get prescription meds, and they don't work either.

Joel and I and Dan come upon the solution together. One of us (I don't remember who) says, "We're goin' in!"

Dan's bathroom is not handicapped accessible like in hotels. But Joel has sawed the bathtub in half so Dan can roll straight into the shower.

First we take off Dan's clothes. Then we carry him onto the shower chair, which is basically a wheelchair with a hole in the seat. We know we're all going to get drenched, so Joel and I get nude too. After we are all in the shower, with water coming down on our heads, I kneel as close to Dan's bottom as a mother has ever been to her adult son's bum. And then (this is not for the faint of heart), I put my finger up his rectum while my Comedy Central husband performs the opening (pardon the double entendre) monologue.

"I know you're up there, Cheney. Come on out. Out ya go. You got Rummy up there too? Come on, you creeps. Out ya go."

Dan begins laughing and laughs so hard the waste flows and we have another successful show. I play the unplugger and Joel stars as the song-and-dance man. Vaudeville has nothing on us.

I grew up in a family that worried about what other people would think of us. I remember my mother didn't want us to wear penny loafers because she was afraid the next-door neighbor, Mrs. Rosenthal, would think Mom didn't care about our arches, so we wore saddle shoes with good support and never got our loafers.

When I heard the phrase "What other people think of me is none of my business," it changed my life.

When you're writing your memoir, if you're worried about what other people will think, it will silence you. It will stop you. It will inhibit you.

And the work will be generic and safe and completely uninteresting.

Give your personal Mrs. Rosenthal some elephant tranquilizer. That will quiet her right down.

Prompt

Is there someone you're concerned about knowing your business? Write them a short letter. Tell them as much or as little as you want.

Write a piece that includes a taboo topic.

CHAPTER 22

Journal, Journal, and Please Journal

Today I found an old guest book from 1994. I couldn't resist thumbing through and reading what people who had stayed with us had written. The first entry was one I had written about our decision to move to the Vineyard year-round. If you had asked me before I read the page how it was moving full-time to the Vineyard, I would have said, "Oh, it was great." And I would have believed that. History is written by the winners, and I guess I had decided it was an easy transition. I did not remember that I had been scared, that I had been ambivalent, that I had been so vulnerable about the move. If I had not kept this guest book, I wouldn't have known how I really felt back then. If you want to write your story, you need to track your journey so you can process it, write it, and heal it. Make sure you date your entries! Because where did that ambivalence and fear go? I'm sure they are inside somewhere, lurking in my cells. Marinating. And those feelings need to be written about to be set free. Because, as Caroline Myss says, biography becomes biology.

Prompt

Go to your journal and pick out something, anything, and expand on it. If you have no journal, go get yourself one. Moleskines are expensive, but they will make you feel like a writer.

CHAPTER 23

You Are Not a Reporter

Just the facts, ma'am. That's journalism. *Who, what, when, where,* and *why* are the five Ws they teach you as the fundamental questions every story has to answer. And all these are important, but in a memoir what's more important is what people *feel* about the facts, how they react to those facts.

This was published in a new magazine on sustainable living:

I just got the most gorgeous wedding invitation I've ever seen. The calligraphy on the envelope is hand done. I know because I spilled some water on it and it smudged. The announcement itself is on hard-stock paper and has a black-and-white hand drawing of the chateau where the wedding will be held. I googled and saw the hotel choices where we would stay, and I'm salivating.

It's not just the classiness of the event that makes me want to go. It's that I love the kid who's getting married. I have known him since he was a boy, and I have always loved him. I love his parents. I love his sisters, and I love his intended. Plus, the wedding's in France and I've never been to France.

Of course I've never been to France. As you know by now, I'm married to the Energy Czar. He has told me time and again how much CO2 planes put out. It's one of his many rants that land on deaf ears. Not mine, necessarily, but what can I do? I can only savor the moment. And this moment is magnificent.

It's 55 degrees and a perfect sunny spring Sunday morning in Chilmark. The Energy Czar and I are sitting by the fire expressing our gratitude for being healthy and just, ya know, life.

Me: We are so lucky!

Joel: We are.

Moment of reverie followed by:

Joel: But ya know, you burn a lot of wood.

Me: I know, and I know it's hard for you, being the conscience of this household and the world.

Joel: The thing is, wood smoke is air pollution. It produces mercury, carbon monoxide, greenhouse gases, volatile organic compounds, and nitrogen oxides. To say nothing of fine particulates, soot, and carbon dioxide. Probably hundreds more chemicals I don't even know about.

Me: OK, OK, I hear you. But I have a theory. It's not based in science, but someday science will catch up and have an equation for this.

Joel: I know. It's your Pleasure Theory. The same one you use for sitting in the sun at high noon. So much pleasure protects you from melanoma. I'm not sure about that one.

Me: Well, yeah, it's the same theory, but I think I can put it in better terms. You agree that everything is energy, right?

Joel: I guess. Mass can be converted into energy, and energy can be converted into mass. You look at $E = mc$ squared, and there it is.

Me: Uh-oh, you're doing that thing again. I don't look at $E = mc$ squared and think *there it is.* I don't look at $E = mc$ squared at all. But let's get back to my theory. The pleasure we are ... well, we *were* getting until you gave me the wood-burning lecture, from this cozy warm beautiful fire gives us energy that we then take in and ultimately will give back out. Somehow everything we do next is affected by that bliss we are experiencing now. So I believe it's actually canceling out any negative effects the wood is doing to us and to the planet.

Joel: I know what you're saying.

Me: Good. So if you take away that pleasure, which I know you call indulgence, then you've got robots — unfeeling, emotionally inaccessible, unevolved, hollowed-out automatons walking around in purified air.

Joel: But pollution is pollution.

Me: I'm not talking about hedonistic living, only-for-our-own-gratification pleasure. I mean being responsible, loving beings — but having some soul food should not be that wrong.

Joel: I'm not saying it's wrong. I love the fire too. It's just that if everyone cut back, which I know they never will, on meat because of the methane, on water waste, on driving stupid big vehicles ...

Me: Easy there, big fella. You can't take people's big cars away from them till they know what harm they are doing. And you can't call the vehicles stupid because then you're calling the people driving them stupid. You're just frustrated because you've been watching the beautiful blue ball die for all the years I've known you, and you've had it. So instead of insulting people, educate them.

Joel: That's the thing. It's too late. I'm afraid it's too late.

The man sounds like a one-issue ogre. He's not. Last week a friend of ours came over with her broken toaster. He worked on it for two hours. She could buy Westinghouse, but he fixed it. He volunteers with kids at Concord Academy; he spends time with anyone who has questions about their ideas for inventions and patents. He's the best, most loving grandfather. Plus, I used to leave my Christmas lights on day and night all year long, and I drive a Volvo, not a Prius. Whenever anyone announces their plans to fly somewhere, he is quick to tell them there are close to a hundred thousand flights in the air every day. And then he gently looks away.

A plane overhead interrupts our conversation. My husband looks up and says with despair in his voice, "Do you realize there are close to a hundred thousand flights in the air every day? Every day, Nance. A Boeing 747 uses one gallon of fuel every second. A flight from Logan to LAX puts out about four hundred thousand pounds of CO2!"

His head is in his hands now.

"It's too late. It's just too late."

I love this man who cares so much about the planet, and I don't like myself for needing to travel to this elegant celebration.

I look at my poor husband, head in hands. I take the gorgeous invitation and slip it inside last week's newspaper.

Now is obviously not the right time. But I won't throw it out. Not yet, anyway.

Prompt

Take a news article and turn it into a personal essay.

CHAPTER 24

Do Not Expect to Be Published: Expect to Be Published

This is one of the most important things to keep in the back of your mind, or even in the front. You may not be unique enough for the publishing company's marketing department. One editor I know came out of a meeting with three twenty-somethings (all guys), having just read a manuscript she thought was great. Their comment? "What's a fifty-something-year-old woman doing with a debut novel?"

On the other hand, there are always new authors of every age and description on the bestseller lists. And out of all the cutthroat businesses in the world, my experience has been that publishing is the kindest. Just bear in mind that if getting a book out there is your goal, then get the book out there. If it's supposed to be a big financial deal, that's not in your control. You do the work, and let the Universe decide what journey you're on.

Prompt

Write your publicist's description of your book, the one that will make your book sell like hotcakes.

CHAPTER 25

Have Two Pockets in Your Skirt, Your Shirt, and Your Jacket

The Buddhist scriptures say, Look within. Thou art the Buddha.

The Christian tradition says, The kingdom of heaven is within you.

The Hebrew sages say, Keep a little slip of paper in one pocket that says *you are everything*. And in the other a little note that says *you are nothing*. Look at both to stay in balance.

Prompt

Write you are everything *on one slip of paper and* you are nothing *on another, and put them someplace safe. Take them out and look at them occasionally, or place them prominently on your writing desk.*

CHAPTER 26

Solitude

Make sure you have some solitude. You may have to set up a little space in the back of your closet or your cubicle at work or your local library. But if you don't get a dose of quiet, you won't get past a certain level of knowing, knowing what you don't know and knowing what your book is really about.

After *The Power of Now* sold 7 million copies, Marc Allen, head of New World Library, asked author Eckhart Tolle why he thought his book had become so popular. Tolle replied (now listen to this): he waited for every sentence to emerge from presence.

For myself, I started learning about presence by practicing the word *no*. It's only two letters. It shouldn't be that hard to pronounce. But it's not the pronunciation I'm having trouble with. It's saying it. To you.

My conditioning began, just like yours, when I was in diapers. *No* had a negative connotation. No! don't touch that radiator. No! don't run away from me in the park. No! Don't go too close to the water.

Then *no* moved on to *no thank you*. Would you like more lima beans? Would you like to go visit Uncle Irving? Would you like to go see that nice dentist who gives you a red lollypop?

The *no* I'm nervous about now has to do with the inner hermit I found lurking in my cells during the many isolated months of pandemic quarantine. (I'm writing this as the threat of Covid is receding.)

If I had to use a term to describe myself pre-Covid, at the top of the list would be *social butterfly*.

I love people. I love parties. I love noise. I love music. I love dinners. I love potlucks. I love eating with people. Talking, laughing, discussing, arguing, singing, dancing, just plain being with my fellow beings.

But something shifted in those early months of staying home and learning to be with my Self. It turned out I liked my own company. The bigger surprise was time. It slowed to a lovely crawl.

And the biggest surprise: I loved the quiet.

I've always been a reader, but with everything always pulling me in all directions, I would start articles, stories, even books and somehow not get to finish. The distractions were just my way of life. I never complained because I was happy. If it ain't broken don't fix it, right?

Well, maybe it was a bit broken. Because when I had a year of no plans, no expectations, no folks bursting through the door with a giant, "Hello, anybody home?" (which I always loved), I not only finished books, but I wrote some and just plain slowed down.

I sometimes do a guided meditation in which the teacher, Mooli is his name, says to bring your sense of attention to presence. Don't worry about all the thoughts. You don't have to make an effort or go anywhere to notice. There is no place you have to be. There is nothing to do. Just the natural feeling of being. Stay only in the noticing. Don't follow any thought. Just be here.

I've been meditating for years, some years spent *trying* to meditate, some years actually meditating, and many making up menus for my catering business that I would use...if I had a catering business.

But this past year, with nowhere to go and no one interrupting me, I have managed to sit more often and to let the compulsive thinking float past, and to begin, as Mooli directs, to notice.

What I've noticed is...*everything*.

I have taken the time to watch the habits of birds at the feeder. In the past they were some kind of movement out the window. I filled the feeder, but I don't think I spent real time watching the guests arrive and their very specific pecking orders, their rituals, their personalities. Blue jays are aggressive, and the crest on top of their heads is affected by their moods. When they're excited the crest is fully raised. When they're eating with other blue jays it flattens. And sometimes it goes sideways. They haven't told me what's going on there yet.

The chickadees say *chickadee-dee-dee*. But they add more *dees* when the cats are around. It must be their nervous call.

I used to think the expression "it's like watching paint dry" meant it was something not worth watching. But now it means noticing, a much worthier endeavor.

This new life where I have sat in the room across from my husband for two hours without speaking, both of us engrossed, each in our own worlds, is magic I didn't know existed. I thought you had to talk. Now I look up and see what Joel looks like when he doesn't think anyone is looking.

My kitchen control freak has given way to sharing the space and trusting that this guy who I never thought would know a shitake from a parsnip might be more than a sous-chef and clean-up man. We are cooking side by side.

So many gifts came from what has been for so many a nightmare.

I am filled with gratitude but also an increasing dread. There are more cars on the road than I ever remember there being in April on the Vineyard. More people who have moved here year-round who are nothing but temptations to socialize. And as we open up the new world, I don't know if my old person and my new person can stay in some kind of balance with each other.

On the one hand, I don't want to go anywhere. On the other (and thank God we have two hands), I think I will get a twinge of "but what about me?" if you have a dinner party and I don't get invited. Then again, why would you invite a person who doesn't want to go anywhere?

I'm practicing *no*, but I'm also trying to figure out a limited edition of *yes*.

Prompt

Write a short piece on what you feel about solitude. And about how it felt or might feel to return to the social world.

CHAPTER 27

Perspective

We have distorted memories. We tend to remember how we felt, not what actually happened. Here's an example of a story in which what transpired might be remembered differently by those involved, depending on the person.

My son Dan knew just how to get to me. We had moved to a fairly conservative neighborhood where the lawns were groomed and the cars in the driveways were brand-new. We had two funky old clunkers, and the paint on the front door was peeling. My husband and I both worked, and raking every last leaf that fell from every last tree wasn't our priority, which is what I had to tell one neighbor when she showed up with plastic leaf bags saying, "These are for your leaves." No one had welcomed us with the traditional pie or the backyard wine spritzer meet-and-greet. So I decided I would invite them in and dispel their fears about the hippie couple and let them see our cozy inside life. The fact was, maybe we were kind of hippies. In those days I listened to everything the *Whole Earth Catalog* had to say. Cancer was going to be Big Business, and they would intentionally never find a cure. Never combine certain fruits with certain vegetables; they release enzymes that cancel each other out. Instead of antibiotics, the way to get rid of yeast infections (which had become my health nemesis) was to mix yarrow and goldenrod and keep it refrigerated for daily douches.

So there they were, four very uptight women sitting at my round oak kitchen table with the homemade ginger scones I had baked and mint tea I had brewed from the wild mint growing on my windowsill. Just then, my thirteen-year-old came home from junior high, made a beeline for the fridge, turned to me, pointing at the large jar filled with yellow liquid, and said, "Mom, is this ginger tea or your crotch infection stuff?" So that took care of that.

At least that's my version of the story. If I were to have asked Dan years later, he probably would have had a totally different take on what happened. Maybe the ladies didn't even understand or hear him. Or maybe he never even said it.

There was another time when he was fourteen and we were having important company — meaning I was hoping to impress the fancy people. I must have spent a fortune on fresh flowers. I bought the most expensive cheese, and I had my husband vacuum (he's a better vacuummer) every corner of the house so they would think we were, if nothing else, immaculate. The important people arrived, and everything was going swimmingly until Dan, who had as much anger as a six-foot-two boy body could hold and who knew that I had been nervous about this social event, ambled into the room with a friend and said at top volume, "Well, at least you didn't have a mother who, when you said you had a headache, responded with 'Kids don't get headaches.'" I looked at my guests' faces and wasn't sure if they were horrified or maybe, God willing, hadn't heard him.

Later I said to my rebel child, "That's terrible! Did you have a mother who said that?" By then he was back to his sweet self and under his breath he kind of mumbled, "Well, you only said it once."

I probably never said it, but that's my story. If he had ever written his memoir, he could have written about that bad mother all he wanted.

You get to choose which stories to tell and how to tell them. You can say, "This is what I remember," or, "It was something like this..." It's not a court trial. You did not take an oath. It's *your* life. Your perspective. Your truth.

Prompt

Write a piece two ways, one from your perspective and one from someone else with a completely different perspective. Try two perspectives woven into the same story in which the two people are not hearing each other.

CHAPTER 28

Grief

Your memoir might include the loss of either a family member or a close friend or a beloved pet. Grief is difficult to write about. Trying to be original when writing about a universal topic can be a challenge. It will help to be as specific and authentic as you can.

In his novel *Grief Is the Thing with Feathers*, Max Porter wrote:

> I missed her so much that I wanted to build a hundred-foot memorial to her with my bare hands. I wanted to see her sitting in a vast stone chair in Hyde Park, enjoying her view. Everybody passing could comprehend how much I miss her. How physical my missing is. I miss her so much it is a vast golden prince, a concert hall, a thousand trees, a lake, nine thousand buses, a million cars, twenty million birds and more. The whole city is my missing her.

He never uses the word *grief* but you sure can feel it, can't you?

I wrote a poem after my sister died. She had breast cancer that had come back, and she was in quite a bit of pain. She was my spiritual mentor and best friend. And when she said, "I'm done. I'm ready for the next adventure," I knew she meant it. I was blown away that she had no fear of death and such complete faith in her understanding of the cosmic dance. At first when she was planning her memorial, picking out the music and choosing the crematorium, I was in awe at her courage.

But then after she died, I was bouncing around like a Ping-Pong ball with a dent in it. I went from being angry to wondering why she didn't try everything to thinking, *Wow, she really, really had no fear.* This is what I wrote:

Just when I thought how
surrendered and at peace I was
with your choice to go gently
into this *God* night
a fierce wind rose up in my gut
a hurricane of *now what*
came pouring down the gutters
of my bones
I don't need
poems from friends
to ease the rupture
I don't need
kasha varnishkes
to fill my belly
I don't want a brilliant sunset
that says *there she is*
those hundred-mile-an-hour gusts
burnt my executive functioning
(wires) to a crisp
And all my cells' towers blew apart
I need this pain
I need this broken heart
I need this extreme weather
otherwise
how will I know
what to do
when *your* sister dies?

Here is a poem about grief written by my brilliant student
Philip Howard:

Hello, my name is Grief
and I've come like an unwelcome house guest
an unwanted supplicant in need
an unfavorite uncle that just won't leave

an unliked post stuck indefinitely on your feed
a surgeon without anesthesia
unafraid to make you bleed

Here's another piece, by the writer Laura Lentz, the author of *STORYquest: The Writer, the Hero, the Journey*, a workbook for writers, inspired by the stages of the hero's journey:

> I came to witness grief young. I didn't lose a parent or a sibling, like so many of my friends, but I lost my kindergarten teacher because she lost her son — the five-year-old boy who sat directly in front of me in a class taught by his mother.
>
> I kicked his chair every day to get his attention, because I had two older brothers and that's how I got their attention. I made Brian laugh, made cut-out paper glued to other paper for him and finger paints. Sometimes he turned around and flashed his smile that seemed too broad for his small face he would never grow into.
>
> In a horrible twist of fate, this five-year-old boy rode his blue bicycle into the street and was killed. Just like that my daily world of the best teacher ever — the teacher who wore her heart outside her thin cotton dresses and was never short on love and hugs — was shattered.
>
> And the desk in front of me stayed empty for the rest of the school year.
>
> There were no grief counselors then for anyone. I'm certain it was my mother who gently lit a cigarette, exhaling the impossible news toward the brown tobacco-stained ceiling, because my father pushed grief aside like a monster at the door with an open mouth.
>
> My father's way of dealing with grief was with dead bolts and tools, to lock the monster out, and his way of curing my mother's sadness was to build something for her or get out a wrench and tighten everything that had become loose.

That was the same year when my mother's grief over leaving her beloved city for the country a few years before caught up with her, and the trees our builders had stripped from our land against her wishes made her cry daily, and I was going to school every day to an endless stream of substitute teachers and an empty desk in front of me, carrying grief back and forth in my metal lunch-box.

I became an early student of grief and how we carry it.

My father brought in railroad ties and soil and built my mother large gardens on our acre where she could plant seeds and push bulbs into the earth.

When I was cleaning my desk recently I found a yellowed, cracked, typed note from over fifty years ago given to parents at the close of my kindergarten year, with these typed words — "this has been a challenging year for all of us."

And it made me think of all the grief the world is enduring now, and all the joy and all the hope that walks side by side with the grief, inviting the grief-stricken back to the light of the world.

I'm writing this today to tell you we all have empty desks in front of us, missing people who have imprinted us forever, now gone.

Who can understand why those we love are taken from us, by death or by the wave of grief that sweeps them to a distant shore?

I know this for sure — this is what we came here to learn — how to reconcile that we are mortal beings learning how to release the people we love, the homes we love, even the land we have come to love and revere as the oceans rise and the weather shifts.

What if the whole plan for our earthly existence is to learn to love and release, love and release — not just to love small, but to love big, to love each other every day in our bodies ... and then when we are separated, to learn to love beyond the bodies?

We need new words for grief and love that exist beyond the boundaries of time and space. Perhaps cell by cell we are remaking each other every day, through memories and story and art.

Perhaps the language needed for this experience of loving and releasing needs new sounds, new words, new notes for a new song.

We are all the same choir, ready to open our throats and reconnect our broken and mending hearts to each other.

Prompt

See if you can write a song, a poem, or some kind of prose about grief.

CHAPTER 29

Wear Your Heart on Your Sleeve

In memoir you can't use subtext and hide truth. If you're gonna do this, you're gonna have to deal with some tough emotions.

Most of the participants in my workshops are women. But once in a while a guy shows up. His sister-in-law gave the workshop to him as a gift and he thought it'd be a lark. Or his daughter gave it to him, hoping they could have a conversation about something real for once. Or his mother gave it to him because he had given it to her and she had such a powerful experience she wanted him to have one too. Anyway, these guys often arrive a bit cavalier and, for some reason, one particular prompt breaks them in half. They end up sobbing and leaving with their hearts on their sleeves, the hearts that before the workshop had been hidden under layers of cement. The prompt is: "My father never told me..."

In response to this prompt, hundreds of men fill in the blank with "that he loved me." I've gotten thank-you notes from mothers and sisters and daughters and even the men themselves, telling me how their lives changed once they were able to admit how painful it was growing up with fathers who couldn't express their vulnerability, couldn't express their love. Lots of these men added, "I know he loved me in his own way, but..."

Prompt
Write a short piece titled "My Father Never Told Me."

CHAPTER 30

Write the Blood on the Page

This was what my editor Lary Bloom from *Northeast* magazine, who was one of my most important cheerleaders and writing mentors, said when I told him what had just happened in New York: "Go home and write immediately." But I had just come home ashamed and wounded from being fired from my first big writing job in the big city, and my response was, "There's no way. My heart is broken. I can't write anything now."

He said, "Go home and write it." I said, "Lar, I can't. It's too close." He pushed. I pushed back. I finally went home and found a way in by using the "Day 1, Day 2..." method, and it got me started. And when I finished, I realized how powerful it is to write when you're in the middle of a tragedy.

There's something about writing in the present tense and the present time. When you read what you've written later, you will feel the blood on the page. Maybe the writing won't be that great. Maybe it will need reworking, but the emotional immediacy will be there. And if you wait, it might be lost or softened. Write during tough times, write during weird times, write during scary times, write in the middle of personal transitions, write during uncertainty, and definitely write when your heart is broken.

Here's what I wrote:

Queen Lear

I'm walking up Madison Avenue in the crispy fall dusk, eating sushi with my fingers. I'm smiling. I'm smiling because it's my favorite food, my favorite weather, and one of my favorite streets in the city. I'm smiling because there are flowers on my desk from friends who celebrated this coup I am living. I'm smiling because I have a desk. And soon I will have a paycheck and I will walk into one of these little shops and actually buy something.

I am an editor at a glitzy women's magazine. I have the combination to the locked executive ladies' room. I have my own secretary. I have an insurance package that includes dental *and* mental.

"You saved us!" my husband, whose financial portfolio was hovering on empty, had bellowed into the phone when I called him after the interview. "You are amazing. You are beautiful. How did you do it?"

"I didn't do it," I said. "It was *bashert*," as my Yiddish-speaking grandma would have put it. In my house, *bashert* was the blanket explanation for God's imperfect design.

Here's how it all started. It was summer, and I was sitting in my muggy kitchen in West Hartford. It was a Tuesday. I was waiting for a phone call about a part-time teaching job I was sure I would get and even more sure I didn't want. I picked up the receiver and out of the blue called *Lear's*, a women's magazine that had bought two stories I'd written.

Lear's, according to vicious trade gossip, was Norman Lear's spurned wife's divorce settlement project, a slick magazine "for the woman who wasn't born yesterday," a euphemism for women over fifty. "What I need," said the senior editor whose name was third from the top on the masthead, "is a good line editor." "That's me!" I screamed, practically jumping through the receiver, knowing as soon as I hung up I had to find out what a line editor was. "Bring your résumé and a body of your work," she said. We agreed on Thursday at 11:00.

Résumés, like sonnets, have a specific form, but unlike sonnets, they are only part of the poem. Résumés are lists, lists of jobs that must connect and show increased power and responsibility.

They can't include "Got heavily into whole wheat and bran, 1973 to 1975." "Cannot sew but understand fabric." "Never took offspring to Disneyland in California but did take them to *Eraserhead* at Trinity." They also can't have you jumping from job to job or doing three at the same time or having no job for a decade here and there. In fact, on a résumé there can be no here and there.

I switched all the hippie-dippie stuff with the teaching jobs, which were on the bottom, and put those in the middle, and then I added anything literary I could find and put that at the top. It's astounding how professional one can look on heavy paper stock.

Credentially correct, I marched my totally impressed body into the executive offices of 655 Madison Ave.

New York is a harsh mirror. As soon as I get off the train, my hair frizzes, my thighs dimple, my skin pimples, and my skirt grows six inches longer. I am always a fashion decade behind in New York City. In the Big Apple, I am an overripe Seckel pear.

The senior editor is generous and kind-spirited. She puts me at ease and lets me know that there is a job and that she wants me to get it. "What did you bring me?" she asks, smiling. I reach into my borrowed leather briefcase and hand her the story I had written for *Northeast* magazine about making an appointment and then going through the humiliating and scary experience of an AIDS test. "No," she says, shaking her head vehemently. "Frances can't know you had an AIDS test. What else?"

I pull out last year's October issue of *Good Housekeeping*, the one with my dog story in it. She flips through the pages flippantly, turns back to the cover, back to the impressive color photo, and back to the cover again, where a grandmotherly face is framed in headlines that proclaim "Muffins Muffins Muffins."

"Frances can't know you wrote a story for *Good Housekeeping*," she deadpans. I say with firm resolve, "I don't even know anyone who reads such middle-American muck." A pang of duplicity. The magazine for the woman who was born yesterday, for the woman for whom a good blueberry muffin is tantamount to a good sexual fantasy and certainly as vital as a good explanation of gene-splicing. A magazine that sits proudly on my dentist's waiting-room table. A magazine for which I am suddenly willing to share Frances's contempt.

"What else have you got?" she asks.

I show her a few more stories and my ivory-colored résumé. She nods approvingly and says, "Now you're gonna meet Frances. Your timing is perfect. She's having a good day."

Frances Lear's office is like a Hollywood set. Huge windows that overlook Sixtieth Street, wall-to-wall Berber carpeting, cushy couches, huge black-and-white glossy photos of glamorous models strewn about, a desk covered with importance. Frances is on the phone. She stands behind her desk, looking petite and corporate, clearly a woman who answers to no one.

My prior knowledge of the actual person Frances Lear is taken from a piece done by *Spy* magazine, a piece so ugly, so vicious, so unfunny, I remember automatically thinking if I ever met her I would love her unconditionally. I also know about her from two articles she herself has written in her own magazine, one about being bipolar and one in which she wrote, "I was born without a sense of humor. I do not know how to do humor, nor do I always recognize it. It occurs to me when I am not laughing and everyone else is that it may be harder to be a member of the audience than to play it." I remember feeling her pain and wondering who she was. The last thing I know is that Norman Lear, her ex-husband, went to Weaver High School in Hartford (the same school as my mother).

Her hand is so small in mine and she looks so little, I blurt, "You're tiny!" She bristles, and I realize that only I, who grew too tall too soon, would consider "tiny" a compliment. I pick up the chill and berate myself in the millisecond I have to recover. "No," I say, "I mean your presence in the magazine is huge. I thought you'd be at least six-three and a half." She relaxes, smiles, and comes around the desk, ushering me onto one of the sink-in-and-never-leave couches. She pulls a chair very close to me, looks into my eyes, and says, "So why do you want to work for *Lear's*?"

I am ready. I say, "I feel as if I've been in on its inception. I've been watching its struggle and watching its growth. I know what the magazine needs."

"What does it need?" she asks.

"Humor," I answer. "You guys have to lighten up. You're angry. Too angry." I tell her that I think she has chosen an untapped market and that women all over the country are ready for a magazine of their own that would address the issues she is addressing but that I think they need balance. Then I say, "Can I ask you a question?" "Sure," she says. "What do you think of the David Dinkins thing?" It is the day after Dinkins was elected mayor. "You know," she says, "I used to be so political. When I was young I marched up Fifth Avenue for civil rights. I marched for everything. But since this magazine, I've had no time. I don't even know what's going on anymore."

"Well," I say, "it's your baby. You're nurturing your baby."

She looks at me in amazement and says, "Who are you?" I look at her and think here's my chance to fill in the spaces, give her the subtext of the résumé. But I wonder if she really wants to know who I am.

We talk about a bunch of other things, very few having to do with the magazine industry. Then, in the middle of a sentence, she reaches over and gently pushes a clump of hair off my forehead, the same clump my mother always pushes. "Let me see those pretty eyes," she says. I love it that she touches me. I can work for a person who isn't afraid to touch.

"I assume you can do captions, titles, and decks," she states, glibly. I know what titles and captions are, but I think decks are things people build onto their houses with their home equity loans. Usually I am pretty honest about admitting when I don't know something. But a little voice inside says, *This is not the time for honesty.* So I gulp and nod yes and beads of guilty sweat start gathering above my upper lip. We talk about the magazine some more, and then she asks, "So what do you think you can do for me?" I think about what I do best and what the magazine needs most, and I say, "I can make you laugh." Without skipping a beat she says, "I want you near me. I want to brainstorm with you. I want to work with you. Go negotiate your salary." In seconds I am back in the senior editor's office talking numbers beyond my ken. She assures me, "You'll be in the seventies before long." Does she mean the block? The age? Seventy, as in thousand? Dollars? I suddenly must be a grown-up.

"Does this job have a title?" I ask. "My mother will need to tell her friends."

"Frances is creating this job for you," she says with charged seriousness. *President of the Entire Publishing Business*, I am thinking. *CEO of all Women's Issues in the World? Queen Lear?*

Then she says, "For the Monday-morning meeting, bring ten new ideas, and bring the names of ten famous authors you would like to see write for us. You will take them out to lunch with your expense account." I think I have died and gone to heaven. I'm going out to lunch with Margaret Atwood and Maya Angelou? I'm sitting across the table from Michael Dorris and Louise Erdrich? "Please pass the salt, Mike. So, Lou, baby…"

Then I am told I have to meet one more person and am immediately ushered into the office of the executive editor — Myra Appleton, number two on the masthead.

I am flying. She is steaming mad. She is wearing a wonderful plaid rayon shirt and slacks. She's my age. She's a pro. "So what did you and Frances talk about?" are her first words. I know it had not exactly been a traditional interview so I semi-stammer, "Umm…we talked about politics, research, and humor."

"Can you do decks and titles and captions?" she asks sharply. There it is again.

"They're not my strong points." I gulp visibly.

"Well, that's what we need," she says, authoritatively.

"I can learn," I say, hopefully.

"You either have a knack or you don't," she says, disgustedly.

I start thinking that maybe I haven't been hired after all. Maybe I imagined the whole scene in Frances's office. Maybe this is their Room 101 technique to see if I will break. Then it hits me. This woman's power has been usurped. She is supposed to do the hiring. And as I sit, uncomfortably realizing this, I also realize it probably isn't the first time Frances has impulsively gone over this woman's head. She continues to attack, and I continue to cower.

"I hear you have children," she snaps. "How are you going to just pick up and move here? What are you going to do with your kids?"

Without skipping a beat I say, "I'm going to sell them." Finally, I get her to smile. Then she asks me why they should hire me full-time when they could just continue to buy my stories freelance. I tell her I have just come from standing in line at Waldbaum's with their readers. I know what they want. I say I know they don't want to see Cheryl Tiegs modeling clothes they can't wear. I know they don't want to bake microwave cornbread from scratch. I know they don't want to be condescended to anymore. They want articles about real people, not beautiful people. They want to be informed about relevant issues, but they also want to laugh.

She is listening to me. "So what do you think you can give us?" she asks, finally relaxing a little.

I know I haven't imagined the magical moments of the morning, so I take a chance and I say, "This is gonna sound really New Age, but I think I could bring harmony to *Lear's*." The magazine is known for its constant turnover. I really believe I can change that.

She bursts out laughing and then tells me I will be in charge of a new column called "200 Words" (short, short personality profiles) and "The Woman for *Lear's*" (lengthy interviews with women from all over the country). "How does that sound?" she asks. "I'll love 'The Woman for *Lear's*'" I say, but "'200 Words' is not a lot of words. We're talking essence here, but I look forward to the challenge." As she stands she extends her hand, welcomes me, and says she'll see me in a week at the morning meeting at 9:00.

As I am escorted past the impeccable receptionists, I say, "When I am going down on the elevator, if you hear a cross between mechanical problems and New Year's Eve, that'll be me screaming and jumping up and down for joy."

I have a week and three days to prepare for my New York

move. If I think too much about the negative aspects of this impulsive decision, like that I am leaving everything behind, all in the name of fame and seventy thou, I may not do it. If I try to focus on the fact that this is my chance to be a real adult, go to the Big City, make real money, and have real power, power I make a silent promise not to abuse, I can keep packing.

I arrange for a friend to move into my house and feed the cats and the dog and water the plants and save the mail and make nice to the moldings because a house knows when it's been abandoned. Dan will stay at the Tragers', Josh is already in college, and Joel is temporarily working in Philadelphia. Then I go to the library and study the back issues of *Lear's* and make lists of ideas and writers and more ideas and more writers. Then I go to my sister's and borrow all the corporate clothes she has, and then I pack my things and I move to the Big Apple. A friend of mine in the city says I can live with her for a few months until I find my own place. The night before my first day of work my husband and I go out for blond pizza on Columbus Avenue. It's the best pizza I have ever tasted. We walk back to the apartment, and my husband re-irons my linen outfit for me. I spend the night trying to fall asleep.

Day 1

One of the things I was going to tell them at the morning meeting at 9:00, along with reading my lists, was that I thought they should target the thirty-something women in the suburbs — that they are also the women who weren't born yesterday and that they have no magazine of their own either. But there is no morning meeting. Around 11:00 one of the male secretaries comes into my room with a huge black leather loose-leaf notebook, opens it up to the chairs section, and tells me to pick out furniture for my office. Around noon a features editor comes in, introduces herself, and gives me pages of material on the "200 Words" column I am to write. She says, "Just use the notes in the folder, check the format from the December issue that's about to go to print, and write two pieces on these two women. Sorry, there's no computer for you — just use the typewriter." And she leaves. One of the secretaries tells me the editor who wrote the first and so far only "200 Words" column was fired last Monday.

The typewriter has no margins, so I spend most of the day fixing my typing. I am afraid to leave for lunch because I think maybe the meeting has been rescheduled. I finish the two pieces, but the editor has gone home and her office is dark. I don't know what time people work to, so I don't leave until 7:30. By then I have a migraine, but I still smile all the way up to Ninety-Sixth Street.

Day 2

A notice comes around welcoming Nancy Aronie as writer-slash-editor. That's how I know what I am. Another notice gets dropped on my desk with my assignment for the January issue. I have four two-hundred-word pieces, on Yves Montand, Jesse Jackson, Giovanni Agnelli, and Mel Gibson.

I go into the managing editor's office. The managing editor for this women's magazine is a man. I ask him if I am supposed to interview these people or use material from other pieces. "Hey, if you can meet them," he says, "go for it." I am on the phone all day talking to Yves's agent in Paris, who is arranging a phone interview from Japan for me. Jesse's people tell me it will be impossible to meet him. I beg and say if I could just ride in the car with him for twelve blocks, at least I will have made some human contact, and then the piece can be written from my heart instead of from my head. They say they will call me back. Mel is somewhere making a movie, and he won't arrive in time for my deadline. The public relations guy at Fiat says Giovanni is coming to America to throw a huge party on the rooftop of the Waldorf for his top Fiat dealers from all over the world. The party is Thursday. He says, in a thick Italian accent, "Becoze you arrre so charming, I will messenger an inveetation to you."

The features editor comes down to my office with my pieces

on the two women, the activist from Cleveland and the judge from DC.

"Did you look at December's '200 Words'?" she asks.

"Yes," I answer.

"Well, look at them again. These aren't quite right."

She hands them back to me. I reread the "200 Words" column. It feels like I have gotten the format. I decide to call the two women myself and interview them. I am pleased with the material I get and begin my rewrites.

In the kitchen I am popping my popcorn lunch when suddenly there are women swarming all around me. One of them extends her hand in a hearty welcome. The rest become silent. "Hi, I'm Jane Weston," or at least that's what we'll call her, "and you must be Nancy Aronie, the new editor."

I smile and nod and go back to my popping. But another one asks, "Where are you from?"

"Connecticut," I answer.

"No," she says, "I mean, what magazine?"

"No magazine," I answer, innocently.

"Well," one of them says, recovering from the shock, "what have you been doing?"

I'm still picking hayseeds from between my toes but the silence is so loud, I finally get it. "No magazine" was the wrong answer. There were several right answers. *Elle* would have been a good one. There they all are, waiting to hear what I've been doing. I'm looking at their desperate interest, and I am torn between doing a *Saturday Night Live* bit — "I've been shopping at the Crown, sautéing my slivered almonds in a nice garlic butter, and driving carpool" (spoken, of course, in a thick Long Island accent) — and bursting into tears, admitting I am an impostor, a fluke, a lark. I am tempted to bolt. Instead, I tease, "It looks like you guys want a really good answer. I'll come up with something. Meet you back in here at 3:20." And then I bolt. Once behind my closed office door, I am sad to have seen them so hungry but sadder that driving carpool, to them, has no value.

Day 3

My invitation to the Waldorf arrives. Audreen, the senior editor, proudly marches me into Frances's office. "Tell her!" she beams. "Go on, tell her," as if I've won the lottery. It is the first time I've even seen Frances since my interview. "How did you do it?" Frances shrieks. "A black-tie party with the sexiest, wealthiest man in Italy!"

"What am I going to wear?" I implore.

"What are you going to do with your hair?" she jokes. For a second I am back in the warmth of the Chosen Ones in the middle of Frances's elite inner sanctum.

I write the piece on Yves Montand. I turn in my rewrites on the two women. It doesn't look like I'll get to meet Jesse, so I begin the one on him. I go out to lunch because Frances has just made me feel like hiring me has been her cleverest move and I'm feeling oh-so-New-York. I walk around the neighborhood, grinning that I am a part of this hustling, bustling hub of everything creative and meaningful that has ever been produced, written, sold, designed, imported, exported, and reported. Where if you want a cappuccino no one ever says, "We're sorry. Our cappuccino machine is broken. How about some instant Sanka?"

I walk back through the huge tinted glass doors of 655 whispering to myself, "I work here." I am getting on the elevator and going up to *my office*.

The executive editor pokes her head in and asks, "How's it going?" I tell her, "It's going great, but I could sure use a computer. This typewriter is an antique. A broken antique, actually." "You don't have to type your own stuff," she says. I feel foolish that I didn't know that. They said they have someone to drive me home when I work after dark, so of course they have someone to type my work if my machine is broken. Silly me.

Day 4

I bring my black wool minidress and my only pair of heels in a bag to work. I will change in my office for the party, which is at

5:00. I finish the piece on Jesse and hand it in. I finish the story on Mel and hand it in.

About 4:30, Frances goose-steps to my office and does an about-face into my door. She is holding my stories on the women and shaking them at me. "Have you read the December '200 Words' column?" she bellows. "Yes, I have," I say. "Well, read them again," she orders, then pauses, looks me in the eye, and says, "and do something about your hair." I look in the mirror at this hair that has so riled her. The '60s, when I ironed it, and the '70s, when I paid many dollars to have it straightened, I could understand, but it's the '80s and curly, frizzy, fried, dead hair is in. It's my only "in" thing, and she's offended. Maybe it's the piece on Jesse. Or maybe she's just having *a bad day.*

I dress for the party, fighting back tears. I walk down the four flights of stairs, talking to myself: "You know, before you came this woman was not a healthy puppy. If she doesn't recognize the gift you came to give her, it's her loss. You still leave with everything you came with plus an experience, a lesson, a story to tell. You can still write, you still have the best husband, you still have two great sons, you still have your precious mother, your beautiful sister, your loving friends, a house with heat, and your hair, Hartford hair though it may be." My spirits lift as I glide up to the Waldorf rooftop. There are five raw bars and nine buffet tables covered with caviar and thinly sliced aged *boeuf.* Waiters are carrying platters of hot stuffed everything. I'm happy my waitressing days are over. I pluck a prosciutto melon ball and check the crowd. All the women are French and four-foot-eleven, and all the men are Italian and five-seven. I am towering over everyone, and my dress is too casual. In West Hartford this is a formal dress. Here it is appropriate only for an ophthalmologist's appointment.

The place is packed, and I'm trying to find the star by a Xeroxed picture of him I found in the *Lear's* library. I see a lights-camera-action scene happening in the lobby outside the main ballroom. There is a receiving line with Mr. and Mrs. Agnelli, and the media are in full klieg-light regalia. I slip out the door and come back, sliding into the line unnoticed. When I get to him I introduce myself quickly. I get a short interview with him. He is accessible, charming, and gorgeous. I leave satisfied with a night's job well done.

I have an appointment to see an apartment in the East Village, very east. I walk past a park where homeless people are living in corrugated boxes. Junkies are nodding on every corner, creeps are selling crack and other sundries, and the neighborhood is strangely deserted. People are afraid to go out, and people have no place to go in. The contrast to where I have just been is startling. I am relieved that the apartment is too small.

I can't wait to get to work. Frances is going to love my interview with the sexiest, wealthiest, most powerful man in Italy. I am pleased with the way I have paced my work this week. Everything is done except the "200 Words" on Giovanni Agnelli, which I am sure will practically write itself. I am there an hour before the bigwigs. At 11:30, Frances comes down to my office. She doesn't look at me. "Come with me, please," she says, soberly. I follow her, thinking *uh-oh* and *hmm*. My heart isn't beating a foreboding beat. I'm more curious than worried. She closes the door behind her, mechanically puts her arm around me, and says, "It's not going to work." *What's not going to work?* I wonder — *the office? The desk? The leather chair?* She proceeds to tell me.

"You're a brilliant writer who can get a job on any magazine in New York City tomorrow." I say, "I'm not looking for a job," to which, if she had had a sense of dark comedy, she could have replied, "Oh, yes you are." But instead she says, "I'm really sorry."

"It's a good thing I didn't find an apartment," I say dumbly. "I took that into consideration," she says, smartly. "Well, I guess this is *bashert*. Do you know Yiddish?" I ask her. "A little," she says. "Meant to be," I say. "I don't know why I was supposed to come all the way to New York, but there's a lesson in here somewhere," I say, numbly.

"Keep sending us those marvelous stories," she says as she sweeps me out. On my way to get my things, I stumble into one of the editor's offices. "I just wanted to tell you," I say, "I really enjoyed meeting you. I'm leaving." "What?" he yells, outraged.

"Frances just fired me," I say, unable to quite comprehend the last ninety-two seconds of my life. "That's it!" he pounds on his desk. "She's fired seven other people today."

Walking up Madison Avenue I try to feel better, thinking I am not the only one she fired, but it doesn't work. I silently say goodbye to the shops I still haven't shopped in. I try to cry. I say, block after block, "This is very sad. Cry. This is very bad. Cry." But I guess I know I need a safer place than the street to let loose. The minute I get back to my friend's apartment and run a bath and the water comes out a murky rust, I burst into tears. *The pipes are like me*, I think, *rusty and old*. I lower myself into the tub feeling tragically empty.

The drive home to Hartford is funereal. I keep trying to practice what I preach. But it dawns on me that you have to practice before the disaster, not after.

My husband is understanding, my mother and my son are happy I am home, my dog is ecstatic, my cats don't notice, and I am a walking, open wound. The first person I see on my first day back is in line at the West Hartford Center post office. She greets me with hyperbolic gestures. "How's New York?" she roars. The entire post office line is waiting for my answer. I can't do it. How do I say I got fired without telling the whole story? What is the whole story? Was I fired? Am I really back? I mumble some fabrication to make her go away, to make the people in line go away, to make the whole situation go away.

The first days back, everyone in Hartford is wearing polyester baby-blue Nehru jackets. Their conversation is filled with their joyous discovery of *the salad bar*, which has just come to some of our better restaurants. I am cynical. I am fragile — after all, I am an excommunicated queen. I have to call all the people who sent me flowers and champagne.

On Monday I get urgent phone messages from the two top editors. "This had nothing to do with you," they both assure me. Then on Wednesday, a bizarre note from Frances. "What I would do if I were you is write the '200 Words' several times and practice it until you get it right. And send them to me. That is, if you want to. You're cute, Frances." I keep reading the note, trying to understand what it means.

I call Cut & Curl and make an appointment.

I go to the reservoir to try to make some sense out of life. First I see orange and red and gold leaves. Then I hear the ducks planning their winter trip. Then I remember how much I love this place. Then I come home and I look at my son, who will go off to college soon. Then I go to Nanshe's gourmet shop, and Sheila says, "Good timing! We just got your Latvian bread." Then I go to Marty's Mobil, and Muddy says, "Nance, I'm still lookin' for a good deal on a pickup for ya." Then I go to the health club, and Sarah says, "You've got the pool to yourself today, kid."

Then I think how condescending I was to all the good readers of *Good Housekeeping*.

Then I think of how easy it was to erase all memory of my AIDS test, for convenience.

Then I think of how lucky I am that I can make impulsive, gut decisions even when they are wrong.

Then I think, *Since when do I have the corner on the sophistication market; what's a little poly among friends?*

Then I think how lucky I am to have a home to come home to.

Then I think how Mozzicato's cappuccino machine is always working.

Little by little, I start to heal. Little by little, I embrace being home. I cancel my haircut appointment.

After a year and a half the pain is completely gone, but the experience lingers. I am glad I went. I am glad I'm home. And now my grandmother's rationale "everything that happens is *bashert*" has been not only touted but also tested.

I think God's design is not so imperfect after all.

Prompt

No point in waiting for a heartbreak or a disappointment to do this prompt. But I bet you can recall one. And see if you can make it feel immediate.

CHAPTER 31

Timing and Edginess

Are you doing anything slightly off-center or trying another way of being in the world? It's your willingness to be out there on a limb that makes your situation interesting. That and, of course, the way you do the telling.

Here is a story about how I once handled a series of obscene phone calls (back when they were actually a thing; with the internet, they are a thing of the past):

I'm standing at the stove dipping oblong tofu chunks into bread crumbs and frying them. I'm gonna tell the kids they're chicken fingers. My mother did the same thing with liver, only she called hers veal. We knew it was liver, just like my kids will know it's tofu. So I grew up hating veal instead of liver. My kids will not grow up hating chicken fingers, however. They will just have a strange food reality, a legacy passed on from their mother and their grandmother. A food by any other name still tastes disgusting if it starts out disgusting.

The phone rings. I go hello. He goes hello. I go hello again because I can't hear him. He goes can I ... and the next sentence, although beautifully alliterative, sounds possibly obscene. But I still can't hear him so I go hang on, I'll take it in the den. Once in the den I say I'm sorry. I couldn't hear you with the oil bubbling and the kids screaming and the dog yipping. Now hello. He repeats his string of obscenities, and I don't know why I don't just hang up. Maybe I haven't had my fill of obscene phone calls. Maybe I've invested so much time and energy into this one, I can't just hang up. All I know is, I say (and I don't know where this comes from), do you have any idea how women feel when they get this kind of call? Do you even care? There is a long silence on the other end, and I can hear him thinking *hey, this is my call. I'm supposed to ask the questions.* I continue. They are terrified. They start shaking. They don't know if you know them or if you just picked their name at random. Now I'm shaking and wondering if he knows me or if he picked my name at random. I lower my voice to the authority octave and push on. They wonder if you're hiding in their shrubbery. For weeks they're afraid to go out, answer the phone. It affects their marriages, their kids, their work, their sleep. I pause. I wonder if he's still there. Another silence.

Finally he speaks. Are you serious? Is everything you said true? I mean, I didn't know it affected anybody that much. I say well, it does. He says I'm sorry. I say I'm glad you're sorry. He says I thought women liked stuff like that. I say well, they don't. He says I didn't mean to make anyone afraid. I say I'm sure you didn't. He says I wouldn't do anything to hurt anybody. I say I'm sure you wouldn't. He says I didn't think it was such a big deal. I say well, it is. He says yeah I guess so. I say I really appreciate your listening. Just don't do it anymore. Like I'm talking to my son. He goes I'm sorry and I don't know you and I just picked your name from the book. Thank you I say. Thank you for telling me that. That was a kind thing to do. I have to hang up now. He says OK. Later.

We hang up. I walk back into the kitchen triumphant. I am singing "Matchmaker, matchmaker, make me a match" at the top of my lungs. What makes you so happy? my kids ask. I have just twinged an obscene phone caller's conscience and refused to be a victim all in one shot. That's nice, Mom, my kids humor me. I tell them about the call over our meal of fried chicken fingers. Something is wrong with the texture of this chicken, my kids complain. There are lots of leftovers.

The next night during dinner the phone rings. One of the kids answers. Mom, it's for you. I excuse myself from the table. I go hello. He goes hi. I go, Oh dear, it's you. He goes yup. How're ya doin'? Well, I'm eating dinner actually. Oh he says, I'll call you another time. I say Oh, OK. He says bye and I say bye and I come back to the kitchen, the glory of yesterday sobering. I tell the family who it was. This guy's really sick, my eleven-year-old says. I defend him. I don't think so. Maybe just lonely.

The next night and the night after and for several months every once in a while he calls. My kids yell, Mom, it's your obscene phone call guy, and we talk about his new job at Goodrich Tire or his trip to his uncle's chicken farm in Vermont or the possibility of his taking the high school equivalency test, which I encourage.

Could be a good sign. Could be a bad sign. All I know is, liver can be veal, tofu can be chicken fingers, and an obscene phone call can be decent.

Prompt

Write a response you would give now to an obscene text. You can be funny or angry or...?

CHAPTER 32

The One Line

This chapter isn't about the fact that my first affair was with a
girl, although that is a fact. It's about how one spoken line, a few
words, can change a life, a mood, an entire situation.

In the sixties my sister and I met a guy who had started
something called Reality Therapy. The questions you ask yourself
before speaking are: *Is it true? Is it necessary? Is it kind?* We fell in
love with the concept and maybe with the guy too.

Many years later, when Dan started to lose his ability to hold
a fork and to do his own insulin shot, and then started falling
after taking only a few steps, screaming obscenities, I didn't ask
those questions. I said the exact worst thing anyone could say.
I said, "I know how you feel." It wasn't true, it wasn't necessary,
and as I learned by his reaction, it wasn't kind. He was twenty-
two and had been diagnosed with MS, and I was telling him "I
know how you feel"?? Of course I didn't know how he felt, but
what I meant straight from my breaking heart was, "I know how
hard this must be." But even those words weren't accurate. I knew
nothing of what he was going through. I only knew how hard it
was *for me*. I learned after a bit of time and a little shrinkage
that the best thing, the only thing, to have said was, "I can't even
imagine what this is like for you."

In the first few of the sixteen years Dan was sick, my dear
friend Gerry just watched. He saw the relationship up close and
very personal. He listened and he observed and he never said a
word until one day he said the thing that would change everything. He said, and it just about killed me to hear, "Your pain is so
great, Dan doesn't have room for his own."

When I say his words changed everything, I mean I switched

from suffering in front of my boy to taking a huge step back and for the first time listening and letting him have his own experience.

Words that comfort, words that change a life direction, well-considered words, are what Reality Therapy is clearly about.

Once, without realizing it, I somehow said exactly the right thing. I found out how right a few years ago when a young woman came up to me holding a golden velvet scarf, and said, "You won't remember me, but ten years ago you stopped me on Main Street in Vineyard Haven. I had quit my job, closed my bank account, and written my suicide note. You said, 'Oh my God! You are lighting up the whole sidewalk. It might be that gorgeous scarf, but I think it's your energy.' I just want you to know you saved my life, and I want you to have the scarf. I've saved it all these years."

I still can't believe how easily my words had rolled off my tongue without my having a clue that they could have such an impact. And yet I've noticed that a lot of people (and sometimes I'm one of them) *think* the kind thought but don't go the extra mile to express it.

I was in a locker room once and probably unattractively nude when I overheard two women talking. One said, "Can you believe Marianne's cream of mushroom soup last night? Wasn't that amazing?" And the other woman said, "It was the best I've ever had." Now, to be fair, their lockers were right next to mine, but to be completely transparent (no pun on the nudity), I eavesdrop, and this time, even though I had never seen these women before, I guess I felt we three had bonded. After all, what's more intimate than dripping together in our birthday suits? Without skipping a beat, I said, "Well, did you tell Marianne?" They looked at each other like *who the f*** is this lady?* Finally one of them said, "She knows she's a great cook." That's where I wanted to lecture about the difference between withholding and gushing.

And the affair I had with a girl? It was with my college roommate in 1963. The day after, on a long-distance call to my mentor older sister, whom I hadn't seen for a year, I had whispered that I desperately needed to talk to her. I told her I couldn't say it over the phone. Three days later she walked in the door, and after our initial hugs, she said, "So? Tell me!" And I said, "I can't tell you here. We have to go out somewhere." So we jumped in the car and started driving around the neighborhood. "*What* already," she demanded, a bit peeved by this point. I said (gulp), "I'm a lesbian." She said, "Oh, thank God. I thought you were going to tell me you were pregnant." And if that weren't enough to dissolve the twenty-one-story building made of guilt I had been carrying on my shoulders, she said, "Have you even done it with a boy yet?" When I told her no, she said, "Then why are you so anxious to label yourself? Why don't you just do it and see what that's like?"

In just a few chosen words she took away the shame and opened the door of possibilities. And reminded me that if it isn't true and it isn't necessary and it isn't kind, let's just keep our mouths shut. Otherwise, open wide.

Prompt

Write a piece about the one line that you thought to say, that you actually said, or that you wish you had said.

CHAPTER 33

Give Your Story Time to Breathe

Step away from the writing. You need to let it rest. It needs air. It needs space. It needs roots. Send those roots down into the mud. Let them find the trace minerals. You're smothering your book, and it feels a lot of pressure to deliver. It's a partnership. It's not just you. Just like lovemaking, there are two entities, and both need nurturing and time. Don't rush the brush. You know how much better it is when there are two of you in on the act.

Prompt

Set a time for when you will return to your work, and stick to it.

CHAPTER 34

Be an Eavesdropper

Some of your best stuff is going to come from listening. That's why going into public places alone is key. Just lean in and take notes. People say the darndest things, and sometimes when you listen, you learn something that will serve you well when you're writing.

I wrote one of my favorite pieces from almost the exact dialogue I heard. I had gone to a fancy spa by myself. After my amazing facial, where afterward instead of looking fifty-nine I looked fifty-eight, I walked out to the pool and lay down on a chaise, ready to sunbathe and reclaim some of the wrinkles the esthetician had just taken away. As I applied my Coppertone Tanning Oil, SPF 8, I heard the sounds of satisfied spa customers. (What do you call people who have had their spa treatments? Spadettes?) Anyway, four young women came around the corner and sat close enough for me to hear their conversation.

The first one said, "We should go into town shopping after lunch."

And I thought, *Oh, this isn't enough for the rich little shits? Now they have to go shopping?!*

And the next one said, "What about the kids? They'll be getting out of camp."

And I thought, *Oh. My. God. They don't even love their kids!*

And the third one said, "The guys will be getting off the golf course. They can take them."

And I thought, *OMG. They don't even want to be with their husbands!*

And the fourth one said, "There's a new restaurant in town. We should check it out. We could just have a drink."

And I thought, *Oh, the five-star gourmet spa food here isn't good enough? The little spoiled brats have to go into town to the newest hotspot?*

The first one whips out her phone and says, "It's called the Restaurant. It looks totally cool! Listen to what's on the menu. Red wine short ribs with parsnip puree. Does that not sound dee-vine? Oh, and listen to this! White chocolate cheesecake. I love white chocolate!"

I am thinking, *I hate these women. Too young to have this much. This is what's happening with all that hedge-fund money. What's going to be the big surprise for them? They'll have seen everything, done everything before they're even thirty. Oh, it's a travesty. They'll be bored by thirty-one.*

Then the second one says, "Maybe we should go to dinner, just the girls."

I am thinking, *I can't believe what I am hearing. I hate them, I hate them, I hate them. And the poor kids. And the poor husbands.*

And then the second one says, "Wait a minute, I forgot! I have a conference call at three."

And the first one, who started the whole thing, says, "What was I thinking? I've got a report due Thursday. I have to get back to the room."

And the third one says, "I'll take the kids so you guys can get your stuff done."

And the fourth one says, "And it's my mother-in-law's birth-day and she's lonely. I'm going to FaceTime her and cheer her up. So let's bag the trip to town."

And all of a sudden I think, *They work. How do they do it all? The stress of kids and husbands and jobs and reports due! Of course they needed to come to a spa. And they're such good girlfriends. Look at the one who offered to babysit! And the one who's gonna call her mother-in-law. She's thoughtful and kind.*

I love these women. They're like my little nieces. I'm so glad they got to come here for a little relief from their impossible stressful lives.

And then I thought, *Nancy, you really are a sick person.*

Writing the truth about your own shortcomings first makes you feel ashamed and then invites gratitude for catching yourself.

Prompt

Eavesdrop, and start a piece using a line you overheard.

CHAPTER 35

Use Dialogue

We need to hear the direct voices of the characters. They become much more real when we hear their actual voices.

Once Dan was bedridden and I (almost) stopped looking for new healers and old miracles and the next goji berry, Dan and I had extraordinary conversations.

"Mom," he said one day as I lay back next to him on the hospital bed we had recently installed in his room, "did I ever tell you about the personal ad I answered when I lived in Waste Haven?" That's what he called West Haven. When I said no, Dan continued, "Well, the description was something like 'I am six feet tall,'" and here he turned to me with that grin, that grin that made women fall head over everything for him, and said, "You know I like 'em tall. Then it said 'I'm gorgeous. I have long blonde hair, and there is nothing I won't do to make sure you leave happy and smiling.'"

I said, "Oh God, Dan, you didn't."

He said, "Oh God, Mom, I did."

I thought, *Who answers those things?*

He said, "Her place was in a really questionable part of town in an already questionable town. So I go up the stairs and knock on the door. And actually she is gorgeous." Then he stopped. I was lying there next to him looking at him, thinking, *How did his former life end? And look how handsome this guy is and he'll never have a wife and he'll never have kids and he's gonna die young and…*

He said, "Are you sure you can handle this?"

I said, "Dan, have you ever known me not to handle everything?"

"True," he said, "too true." *My son's eyes have gotten bigger, I* thought. *No, he's gotten smaller. Thinner. He's gotten sweeter. He's a raisin.*

When a person is lying in a bed, you can't tell they were once six-foot-two. You can't tell they were once at motorcycle-mechanic school, racing Harleys down Highway 1. You can't tell there was always a beauty on the back. You can't tell they once majored in psychology at Bard College, one of the best schools in the nation. You can't tell anything about anything. You can only be present with this brand-new person with this body that is failing by the minute.

"So what can't I handle?" I said.

"Well," he said, "it turns out she was a *he!*"

"No!" I said.

"Yes," he said.

I said, "What did you do?"

He said, "I jumped up, put my clothes back on, and said, 'I'm sorry. I have to go.' And if it weren't for the fucking cane I would have run out of there."

The cane. The cane ... one of the worst days in my life. Buying a cane in an apothecary, a hot stuffy smelly drugstore with interlocking wheelchairs as if it were a parking lot for the handicapped, aisles and aisles of medicine with all old people shuffling in and out, and my James Dean boy lost in a fog of *What's next after a cane?*

"So what did you say?" I said.

"I said, 'Good luck.' And I left."

"Good luck? You said, 'Good luck'?"

"Yeah," he said, cracking up now. "I actually said, 'Good luck.'"

We hung for a while in silence. Silence became part of our new way of being. Silence that was nice, holy almost. I looked around the room. I remembered bringing him paint chips to decide on what color his prison should be. He would live in this room now, mostly always. So I was determined to make the place a spa. Calming, beautiful, peaceful. He chose an indigo blue, which I thought was too dark, so I got one three shades lighter, knowing he wouldn't know the difference. He didn't. Brian, one of the caregivers' boyfriends, painted stars all over the ceiling. Brian used to bring his bong in and share with Dan. If Dan smoked, I wouldn't, because I had to be on vigilant alert. If Dan said no thanks, then I would imbibe. Brian brought his music into the room and sometimes would stop at the foot of Dan's bed and dance and then shake his head back and forth and say, "You're my hero, man. I couldn't do what you're doing." I loved Brian in those moments.

The multicolored quilt, also with stars, that his friend Erica had given him from my favorite store, Midnight Farm, lay across the bed. I always sprinkled lavender on Dan's pillow so that when company leaned over to kiss him it would smell good.

Candles burning, stars glowing, curtains (that Gerry measured and made on an actual sewing machine) wafting in the breeze, it was a spa all right. It made you feel like whispering.

Prompt

Write a piece using mostly dialogue. Even whispered.

CHAPTER 36

Vulnerability above All Else

We want to like the narrator. We want to feel empathy, sympathy, and we want to trust that the writer is credible. We want to be able to relate to you. We want to identify with you. So be vulnerable. The reader will not think you're nuts if you're emotionally honest. Even if your experience is totally different from ours, and our details are different, and our story is different, it turns out that our samenesses are the same. We all want to be loved. We all want to be held. We all want to be listened to. Your reader will not think you're nuts if you're emotionally honest and vulnerable.

We want you to be a nice person. If in fact you're not, write fiction.

Prompt

Write a story with a mean protagonist, and then slowly let her change.

The only main character of a book that I couldn't stand was Olive Kitteridge. But two things: it was fiction, and in the end of the last chapter she did something that explained why she was so miserable, and I not only forgave her for all the mean things she had done, but I ended up loving her. It took the whole book for me to feel empathy for her.

You are the main character in your memoir. And I want to love you too. I want to think, Wow she's just like me. She's an asshole too. She's made some bad choices too. But how did she get to where she is now? *Show me a road map. How can I get to a new place even with my assholeness?*

CHAPTER 37

Don't Trick Your Readers

Don't write about how much you loved Leo and how heartbroken you are now that he's gone and how your bed is empty and you cry all the time and you think about him constantly and everything reminds you of him. And that you know you'll never recover from this loss and that you're sure you'll be alone for the rest of your life. And on and on ad nauseum, but we're sticking with you because we like you and we feel horrible for you, and then in the last sentence we find out that Leo was your dog. Loving your dog and missing your dog is completely legit, but tricking us into thinking it was your husband is a betrayal. There is a difference between invention and deception. After you manipulate us, we will be angry, and it will cancel out anything good we might have felt about the book.

Prompt

Just for fun (and to get it out of your system), write a trick piece.

CHAPTER 38

Etc. and So Much More

Please don't use *etc.* All that tells me is that you're not willing to do the work. You didn't finish. And please, at the end of a list, do not say *and so much more.* If there's so much more, either give it to me or don't tell me about what I'm missing. Otherwise, I'm just going to be reading and thinking, *What else?*

Prompt

Write a sentence where you make a list, and just when you're tempted to write etc. *add a detail instead.*

CHAPTER 39

Accept the Possibility of Failure

*Rejection slips, or form letters, however tactfully phrased,
are lacerations to the soul, if not quite inventions of the devil —
but there is no way around them.*

— Isaac Asimov

Failure can either devastate or turn into growth, or it can do both. I had been doing commentaries for *All Things Considered* on NPR for five years. I would call my producer and say, "Do you have two minutes?" And then I would read him my piece, and he would say, "Brilliant! Go tape it." And I would drive to Northampton, Massachusetts, the nearest NPR station to Hartford, where I lived, and tape my story. And it would be aired two nights later.

One day I called, and instead of saying, "Great, go tape it," he said, "Didn't you get the letter? You were supposed to get a letter." I said, "Well, I didn't get the letter, Art. What did the letter say?" He hemmed and hawed, and I could tell he was uncomfortable. Finally, he said, "They've canceled a lot of the commentators. And you were one of them." I hung up in shock and started walking from room to room, mumbling. I was just learning about gardening, and I kept repeating, "I'm a dried-up bloom. I've just been deadheaded, but I will grow from this. I will be a bigger flower. I will grow from this. I will be a huge flower." I'm sure I had no idea what I was talking about, but I think the words did their soothing job, and little by little I accepted the loss.

The thing to know about failure is that it happens. It happens that you could work for two years and finally finish your manuscript and send it out. And it might happen that you get no response from fourteen of the twenty-three you sent. And the rest are rejections. Not nice rejections. Form rejections. One-line rejections: We are not accepting unsolicited manuscripts at this time.

But here's the thing. Disappointment doesn't kill you. It hurts. But *you* are *not* a failure! And the book is not a failure. It's a beginning. Ask those who wrote back if they could tell you why it didn't work for them. Some of them might give you answers. Most probably will not.

And then what do you do? You go back to the drawing board. Or you put whatever you had written aside and start again.

I have Cray-Pas, those gorgeous chalky pastel crayons. When I get rejected to the point of thinking, *WTF, why am I bothering?* (and this has happened more than once), I get out some textured watercolor paper and take the indigo crayon and swipe it across the page. And then I smudge with one finger and then I take the orange crayon or the forest-green one and draw a careful line right above the blue, and honest to God, I think I am a genius! I think I'm actually an artist. *Why do I spend any time writing? Look at this brilliance. I was born to do art.*

And after a while I begin to miss words and I creep back to my yellow legal pad or even the computer and I write something, anything, and my fingers remember how much they like what comes out of them. And I'm back.

I don't know what will work for you, but trying another art form, one in which you are not expected to be accomplished, can be very liberating.

Ray Bradbury said, "Any man [I'm sure he meant woman too] who keeps working is not a failure. He may not be a great writer, but if he applies the old-fashioned virtues of hard, constant labor, he'll eventually make some kind of career for himself as a writer."

My friend Jude, who makes gorgeous jewelry, put it this way: "Krazy Glue your butt to the chair." (No, she does not use Krazy Glue for her 24-karat-gold gems.) I think she says it better than Ray, and he was a brilliant wordsmith, for God's sake.

Next time you receive a rejection, remember to use the glue. Also remind yourself that you're a perennial. And you will come back! Bigger, even.

Prompt

Write yourself a rejection, explaining why something didn't work.

CHAPTER 40

Now Let's Talk about Success

Know your own definition of success.

Is it financial? Is it revenge (as in, *I'll show him*)? Is it fame and recognition? Is it completing something?

I ran the Mother's Day road race on Martha's Vineyard, where I live, when my son Josh was nine, which means I was thirty-nine, which means it was forty years ago (that wasn't a typo). The course was 3.1 miles (but who's counting?). I had just started running regularly. And I was slow. During the last mile I was rehearsing what I would say to the reporters when they asked, "How does it feel to come in dead last?" My answer was, "Great! I did it!" Unfortunately, I was third from the last so I didn't get that distinction, but I did get the feeling of exhilaration that comes from success. By no one else's standard had I succeeded, but no one could take away the feeling I had of being a winner!

Prompt

Write about a time when you were a winner by no one else's standards but your own.

CHAPTER 41

Visualization

I never knew there was actually a practice called visualization, but when my husband and I had a business and it was clear we were either going to go bankrupt or miraculously be able to sell it, I thought I had come up with an original idea. Every night before we went to sleep I'd say to my husband, "Picture an oval oak table. There is a bottle of champagne. There are two lawyers, and we are closing the deal on the sale of Aronie Galleries." The first few times I went through my nighttime spiel, he would say, almost snapping, "Nance, we lost $75,000 two quarters in a row. No one is buying this business!" And then I would actually snap, "It is an oval oak table! There is a bottle of champagne! There are two lawyers! We are closing on the sale of Aronie Galleries!" Finally I got him to participate. And we did this just about every night for two months. And guess what? It was a rectangular table, but there were two lawyers. And I brought the champagne. And yes, we sold the business.

So if it's a book you want, what's wrong with visualizing its cover? Your book signing? Your oval oak table? Your champagne?

Of course, visualizing will not write the book. That's the part you have to do. Sorry. The Universe can only do so much.

Prompt

Visualize something you want. Do this every night before you go to sleep for thirty days. Write about the results.

CHAPTER 42

Can I Just Take All My Journal Entries and Turn Them into a Book?

Good try, lazy bones.

The difference between a journal entry and a finished personal narrative is the arc and what it taught you: How did you get from there to here? Where you are now? In a journal entry you're most likely writing what happened. In the narrative you're writing about what you learned from what happened. How did you get from some unlikely place to where you are now? Show us the transformation.

You can certainly use your journal for notes and ideas.

Take those personal entries and elevate them, transforming them into memoir storytelling.

Prompt

Open your journal. Pick out a phrase, and begin a piece using the first line.

If you don't keep a journal, you can just make up a line (and please see chapter 22). And then proceed with the assignment.

CHAPTER 43

Take a Memoir-Writing Workshop

There are so many platforms now with great teachers where you can learn some basic writing skills and get some good practical advice. There's nothing like having writing assignments and a group that's waiting to read them.

But the temptation to take seventeen or thirty-seven workshops might arise. After you have taken three, ask yourself if this is a procrastination situation. You don't want to become a workshop junkie. If your goal is to write your memoir, the only thing to do is to start writing your memoir.

Like the meditation joke goes: What's the best meditation technique? Answer: the one that you do.

Prompt

Write about a writing workshop experience.

CHAPTER 44

Anger

You have every right to be angry at the uncle who molested you, at the mother who didn't protect you, at the teacher who humiliated you, at the boyfriend who broke up with you on Facebook. But if your rage is on the page, you push me away. Just tell the story, and let me be angry on your behalf. Then, if I meet your uncle on the street, I'll kick him in the groin. For you. Because I will care that much.

I wrote about anger all the time because I was living with it (Dan) 24-7. I lectured Dan about his anger his whole life. Probably a million times I said, "If you weren't so angry, your life would be so much easier. You push every possibility of joy away with that rage."

Then one day I read a story about a guy who began to give his Doberman large doses of cod liver oil because he heard the stuff was good for dogs. Each day he would hold the head of his protesting dog between his knees, force his jaws open, and pour the liquid down his throat. One day the dog broke loose and spilled the oil all over the floor. Then to the man's great surprise the dog returned to lap up the puddle. That is when he discovered it wasn't the cod liver oil that was the problem; it was the approach.

I stopped talking to Dan about his anger. I couldn't believe my eyes. Dan was starting to become mellow and calm. One night I said, "Dan, I notice you're not that angry anymore. How did that happen?" And he said in his faltering voice, "I noticed that being angry didn't help anything."

Dan had lapped up the oil when I finally stopped force-feeding him.

Prompt

Write an angry piece. Then figure out a way to say the same thing without anger so the reader can get angry on your behalf.

CHAPTER 45

Stories Grow Right
through the Cement

Once in New York City, walking among the throngs, I looked down and saw a tiny purple flower growing right through the cement. How many people had stepped on that flower? And still, it reached for the light. After all these years of hearing stories of what people have survived, I know people grow through the cement. And it's our stories that refuse to lie down in darkness. We, the tellers, are the survivors who have learned to reach for the light. We are all those tiny purple flowers. In writing your memoir, you are reaching for a sliver of that light.

Here's one of my stories that refused to lie down in darkness:

On my way to visit my son in the hospital, I always felt compelled to look into the room right before his. Maybe it was because the boy inside was young like my boy. Maybe it was that he had a mass of dark hair just like Dan's. But I think it was because there was a beautiful woman — his mother, I later found out — sitting, reading the Bible, lips moving, head down, blonde hair falling across her impeccable Talbots dress, her high heels, her stillness. When we first met she said, "God knows every hair on Dan's head, every cell in his body, every thought in his mind."

I remember thinking, *Uh-oh, religious nutcase.* I tried to put on a pleasant, I-am-not-a-judgmental-person face. "Do you believe in the gospel of Jesus Christ?" she asked one day when we both had to vacate our sons' rooms while the aides with Day-Glo hazmat suits went in to administer the drugs that they told us were keeping our boys alive. I said, "Actually, Jesus is one of our guys. I believe in everything, Jane. I believe in Buddha and Moses and Ram Dass and the Tin Man and Judy Blume and Oprah and crop circles."

One day I suggested we go down to the cafeteria for coffee. Jane said no, she couldn't leave her son. He might wake up. It had been three months since his stroke at twenty-four, a graduate in film from Emerson College. The day we sat by the plastic holiday decorations near the nurses' station, I told her of my Jewish Christmas envy, and she told me about her sweet new husband. She told me how being born again was sustaining her and how she was sure Charlie would get better.

She gave me copies of the films he made in college, and I gave her stories Dan wrote while he was at Bard. Jane said, "Charlie prays with me." I said, "Don't mention God to Dan." And Jane said, "Romans 10:9. If you confess with your mouth that Jesus is Lord, that God raised him from the dead, you will be saved." And I inwardly rolled my eyes.

When your loved ones are in the hospital for weeks and weeks and weeks, intimacy can reign, secrets spill, and friendships form. I began to see Jane's passion and devotion as powerful and beautiful. And I appreciated that she didn't preach; she just quoted. One night she summoned me out of Dan's room and told me they'd decided to pull the plug on Charlie. I held her in my arms, and we sobbed like the sisters we had become.

The next morning, I arrived at the hospital before sunrise. The room next door was dark. On my way home that night, I said, "OK, God, you let Charlie die, so now you have to let Dan live." Have I always talked to God? Yep, I have always talked to God. I just never thought of myself as a religious nutcase. And you know what? Turned out, Jane wasn't one either.

Prompt

Write one of your stories that refuses to lie down in darkness.

CHAPTER 46

Write about Something That Shaped You

I grew up with a weatherman living in my house. Well, actually it was a weatherwoman. My mother was obsessed with the weather. And according to her, there was good weather and bad weather. I can hear her wailing now: *Oh no, it's raining!* As if life were now ruined. *We can't go out. We can't go to the beach. We can't go to the park. We can't do anything. Life is over.*

It took me until I was in my fifties to love weather. All weather. I love the sound of rain. I love the feel of snow. I love the snap of cold, and I love what shedding the weight of clothes in summer does for my lightness of being. Once you recognize the powerful influence that early programming has had on you, it's liberating to make choices based on your own desires and not the ones embedded early on in your little psyche. Those are stories to write too.

It's pouring, and I'm listening. The sky is getting dark, and I am hoping for some thunder. Maybe even some hail. I open the door for a whiff.

How is it possible for the girl who grew up with the repeated mantra *oh no, it's raining* to be so entranced by the sound and the smell and the look of a storm?

I'll tell you how.

About thirty years ago, my friend Ger was visiting. My mother, the mantra moaner, was living with me at the time. It was snowing and my friend was wandering out and coming back in and wandering out and coming back in, dusting off the snowflakes. And one of the times he was in, he said, "You guys have got to come out and see." And in unison, like a Greek chorus, my mom and I said,

"*But it's snowing.*" To which he replied, "That's the point. It's gorgeous out there." Reluctantly, we bundled up, looking as if we had starring roles in *Doctor Zhivago*, and throwing caution to the wind (which actually was picking up), we stepped outside.

Indeed, first in shock and then in awe, we saw that it *was* beautiful. We stood under the eaves, sheltered, and watched the swirling flakes dance and glisten. And because we were dressed for the tundra, we didn't even get cold. We didn't have to voice this, but I know we were both thinking, *How could we have missed the exquisite power and beauty of a snowstorm?*

Many years before I had this paradigm shift, I had an audition to be the weathergirl at Channel 30, the TV station ten minutes from my house. I remember thinking on my way there, *I'm good at impromptu stuff, and I'll wing it and maybe even land the job.* There were several problems even before they gave me the three-by-five index card with all the meteorology specifics in tiny print that I had to memorize.

I didn't get a callback, probably for several reasons. One, I wasn't blonde. Two, I wasn't thin. Three, no cleavage. And four, probably the main reason, I can't memorize. And maybe five, my heart was pounding so loudly it more than likely broke the sound system. But I gave it my best shot.

I remember taking the wand and pointing at the edge of the right side of the map and saying something like, "There is a cold front moving." Then I walked across the floor to the other edge, and I think I said (and I admit this was not professional lingo), "From this side of the map to this other side of the map." I couldn't think of the words *east* and *west*, and I couldn't think of the word *coast* either. Needless to say (but I'm saying it anyway), I never heard back from Channel 30. Not even a "thank you for your courage."

Shortly after I started making peace with weather, I got a grandson. And when he was four, he said he wanted to go sledding. I hated sledding as a kid. Remember, it was *out*doors and cold, and besides, there was a whole lot of weather out there.

But when you have a grandchild your brain insists on forging new pathways. You can't say no. It's your job as Gramma to open your mind, to take risks, to be a role model for saying yes. And I had just turned my back on the word *inclement*.

So I bought ski pants for a grown-up (who knew they had such a thing?) and two plastic sleds, and as long as I kept my mind on the floating marshmallows on top of the cup of hot chocolate we would have as soon as this torture was over, not only was I able to survive, but I actually loved every minute of it.

So as I'm sitting here, celebrating every raindrop, I am imagining what I would say if I got that weather job now.

"Wow! What a gorgeous day! I know I'm not a singer, but I'm just gonna belt out a few bars of 'Stormy Weather,' if you'll indulge me." And then I would break out in song. "Because today is a special day. If you are on your way to work, think of how happy the gardens are to be nourished. Think of the worms that are getting a chance to get out for a bit. Think of the shops that sell umbrellas. Think of the bath that nature is giving the hot and the dusty. If you are home and can curl up with a good book, you can turn off the radio or the television, and the meditative sound will heal your heart.

"You know, folks, I used to hate storms. Rain and snow and sleet . . . and then one day someone turned me around and helped me see from another perspective. I'm not telling you that if it's icy you should enjoy driving bumper to bumper and being stressed that you might not make it home. I understand some weather is worthy of respect. But all my young life, I heard my family complaining that *now everything is ruined because of the rain*. The message also came from the weathercasters. 'Another lousy day,' they would say. Well, if sunshine is the only thing that is gonna make you happy, you're gonna have a lot of not-so-happy days. It's a choice. How many lousy days do you want? Don't we have enough stuff to worry about that we can't control? So enjoy today.

"But get out your mufflers because there is a cold front moving from the West Coast all the way," and I would sashay over to the other side of the map and with great assurance, put my pointer on the edge, and finish with a flourish, "to the East Coast."

Prompt

Write about a behavior that stems from your early programming and that you're ready to change.

CHAPTER 47

Read, Read, Read

Read Alice Munro. Read Louise Erdrich. Read Toni Morrison. Read Tillie Olsen. Read Barbara Kingsolver. Read everything by Geraldine Brooks. Read Alice Walker. Read *Grief Is the Thing with Feathers* by Max Porter (you'll be sobbing after that one). Read *Croc Attack!* by Assaf Gavron (it has nothing to do with crocodiles). Read Grace Paley. Read James Baldwin. Read Carol Edgarian's *Three Stages of Amazement*. Read Alan Watts. Read Kate Feiffer. Read Catherine Walthers. Read Jane Lancellotti. Read Suzy Becker. Read Nicole Galland. Read poetry. Read Lawrence Ferlinghetti. Read Whitman's *Leaves of Grass*. Read Anne Sexton. Read Ogden Nash. Read mysteries. Read fantasy. Read everything by Marc Allen. Read Mirabai Starr. Read Elizabeth Lesser. Read Carol Gilligan. Read Virginia Woolf's "On Being Ill." Read Ram Dass's *Be Here Now* (as you know, this one changed my life). Read Thomas Moore's *Care of the Soul*. Read Eckhart Tolle's *The Power of Now* (deepened my life). Read Flannery O'Connor. Read more poetry. Read Ellen Bass, Sandra Cisneros, Lucille Clifton. And maybe read some memoirs. These are all your teachers.

Underline passages that grab you. Read them again to get the music. Copy their style until you weave a bit of them into a lot of you.

Know that these authors are your mentors.

Prompt

Write a thank-you note to one of your mentors, and try copying their style.

CHAPTER 48

Letters: Write Them

A letter is in fact the only device for
combining solitude and good company.

— JACQUES BARZUN

To send a letter is a good way to go somewhere
without moving anything but your heart.

— PHYLLIS THEROUX

You have a touch in letter writing that is beyond me.
Something unexpected, like coming round a corner
in a rose garden and finding it is still daylight.

— VIRGINIA WOOLF

Some of us grew up writing and receiving letters. There are al-most two whole generations now that may never have gotten a letter in the mail. What a loss, I say.

Dan was friends with Harold Ramis, the actor, director, and writer, a generous and loving soul. Harold would often send Dan a script he had just finished with a note saying "Hot off the press" or "What are your thoughts, Dan?" And I would get to read a Harold Ramis script before the movie even premiered.

Harold and his brilliant writer wife Erica would take us all out to dinner when they were here on the Vineyard. Then when Dan was bedridden and could no longer go out, Harold would bring him takeout and sometimes jump into bed with him. They would lie there talking and laughing.

After the last time they ever saw each other, Harold wrote the following letter:

Dear Dan,

My body is an idiot. It can't seem to do anything right anymore, and the pleasures of the flesh have all been replaced by minor torments and the inevitability of major ones. I know I'm partly responsible for not maintaining it — Rodney Dangerfield used to say that when he died he was going to donate his body to science fiction — but, like life itself, our bodies came without guarantees or warranties, and I know that this miraculous and complex machine of mine will eventually fail me entirely.

I used to look at my body and think, *Hey, you're lookin' good!* And I like to think I wasn't the only one who thought so. But they say vanity is a sin. And the Buddha said that sensual pleasure is one of the Five Hindrances to Enlightenment. So if I can't preen like a peacock, run like a cheetah, eat like a pig, and fuck like a bunny anymore, then what's it for, this lump of meat, this highly evolved bag of water, this body of mine?

And then I looked at you, Dan, whose body is an even bigger idiot than mine, and I remembered: Oh, that's what a body is! It's just a container, the sacred vessel of your mind, heart, soul, and spirit. It's the violin case that holds the sweet music in you. It's the jewel box that holds in folds of silk and velvet, the perfect diamond of your intellect. It's the unbreakable steel vault that holds the riches of your heart. It's the ark of your imagination that can take you anywhere in time and space. And it's the furnace that holds the fire in you, the flame of your Being that still shines bright and hot enough to light your starry room in Vineyard Haven and warm us all.

Thanks for reminding me, Dan. Peace, love, and all good things. What do you think — too sappy?

Harold

Prompt

Write a letter and rewrite it and edit it and rewrite it, and make it the best writing you have ever done. And then maybe even mail it.

CHAPTER 49

Essays

A collection of personal narratives, essays, is one way you can structure your memoir. They tell your story as effectively as any other technique. Anything works if it's coming from an authentic place. I happen to be most comfortable with this particular form. Below are two examples.

The Magic Eye

In the early seventies there was a book being passed around in our circle of friends called *Magic Eye Beyond 3D*. Basically it was a collection of two-dimensional images that each had a three-dimensional image hidden in the middle of the page, called a stereogram. People would look for a few seconds, and their response was always, "Wow! Sooo cool!" Everyone but me. I never saw what they saw. They said you had to be stoned to have it work. So I got stoned. It still didn't work.

It was one of those things, like snorkeling and zip-lining, that other people could do — but apparently my brain and body had made an ancient pact that there were certain places they just weren't going to go.

Once in a while I would try *Magic Eye* again, but to no avail. I got all kinds of advice: *Closer, Nance, pull it closer. Make it so it's totally out of focus. Now pull it back slowly. See the image? It pops right out. You don't see the bunny rabbit? Honestly, you don't see?* Honestly, no, I didn't see. I never saw, and though I always tried to laugh it off, I felt left out, and to be blunt, stupid.

So a few days ago, when I was looking for a different book, guess what popped off the shelf and into my hands? I took it and threw it onto my reading pile. Maybe after forty years, I would give it another try. Maybe my brain had shifted into a new gear. I opened the book slowly and carefully, and for the first time, lo and behold, sitting here all by myself, I got it! A sailing vessel as big as life emerged out of the mass of squiggles!

Why, I wondered, did I have so much trouble back then when just now it came so easily? So I googled *stereograms*, and a whole long explanation of optical illusions came up.

Wikipedia said the visual system is what makes things appear different from reality. According to one expert, there are three kinds of classifications for this phenomenon: physical, physiological, and cognitive. The one that grabbed me was the cognitive because I read that it is the result of unconscious inferences. What unconscious inference could have had such a strong hold on me?

And then I remembered something my father had said when I was about eleven. I was taller than almost everyone my age and even taller than some of my teachers and many other adults. One day my dad took me aside and said, "When anyone walks into a room, you're going to be the first thing they see."

As an eleven-year-old girl, growing faster than the entire male population, and as, well, just an eleven-year-old girl, if I had needed one more thing to feel like I was on display, one more thing to be embarrassed about, one more thing to be self-conscious about, my father had just handed it to me.

After many years of introspection and good therapy, I understood the effect those words had had. Thinking back now, I realize that when all my friends were trying to show me how *Magic Eye* worked, I was probably using all my energy to *look* as if I were concentrating instead of actually concentrating.

I weep for that young girl who must have spent hours, probably years, worried about others' perceptions of her.

Thank God, at some point I heard that fabulous liberator of all liberating lines: *what other people think of me is none of my business*. And I repeated it over and over, and I still use it when self-consciousness strikes.

Since my *Magic Eye* breakthrough, I've shown the book to three people. My ten-year-old grandson got them all within seconds, but the two others, both adults, couldn't see anything but a mass of repetitive designs. Both reported they felt too much pressure from my being there with an expectation. So there it is: the perception of being perceived is not easy.

So how do I explain my recent success? I guess my brain shifted gears, the mantra took hold, and my heart had found some wisdom.

Because if you had been in my neighborhood Monday morning, you wouldn't have had to strain your ears to hear my voice shouting from the rafters: "Wow, sooo cool!"

My Mother Always Said...

Years ago I read a biography of Armand Hammer, the oil baron. In it he said his mother always said, "Make haste slowly." I loved that. But then I remember wondering what *my* mother always said, and I couldn't come up with anything wise and worth repeating. And from that thought, I went directly to, *What will my kids say their mother always said?*

When my kids came home from school that day (they were ten and twelve) I asked them. "When you're grown and living on your own, what will you say your mother always said?" They looked at each other and one of the little wise asses quipped, "My mother always said, 'Eat your tofu.'" True, I had gone radical on our food trip, but "eat tofu" was all they could come up with? That was the legacy I would leave? In all their time living with me, I had never imparted any deep philosophical one-liners?

I took a magic marker and wrote on a piece of paper, "As Armand Hammer's mother always said and Josh and Dan Aronie's mother *began* to say, *Make haste slowly.*" And I taped the paper to the refrigerator.

I started asking people the same question. My friend Margo

said one Thanksgiving her sister-in-law called her and pronounced, "You're hosting the holiday this year." Margo hung up and was mortified. Her sister-in-law was wealthy and had a huge house. Margo was broke and lived in a tiny space. She called her mom wailing. "I can't do this. How am I going to do this?" And her mom said, "Honey, is there any way you can get out of it?" And Margo said, "No, I can't get out of it!" And with that her mom said, "Well, if you can't get out of it, then get into it!" I loved that one too!

My mother-in-law always said, "There's nothing common about common sense." So here I was trying to come up with something weighty my mother always said and starting to resent the fact that there was nothing. And then I got real. I remembered that the woman had three jobs. She didn't have the luxury of always saying something meaningful to her kids.

I remember envying my friends whose mothers were home in their immaculate suburban split-levels. But my mom got up every day and went to work. She made payments on her Nash Rambler. She put my clothes on layaway at Casual Corner. And she did all this without one complaint. Ever.

Still trying to think of a *Make haste slowly* kind of advice, I remembered being in her apartment on Sundays, her only day off. She lived in a building with a bunch of gossipy widows. And one by one, they would come visit her. One whispered, "Did you see Lucille's gentleman's caller leave this morning? That means he stayed all night." And instead of being shocked and ready to pass on the evil little tidbit, my mother said, "Ooh, lucky Lucille." Then one tried to gossip about another neighbor, and my mother interrupted before the woman could get out her juicy delicacy. "Doesn't Martha's hair look great?" I watched her deflect their stories time after time, and I knew she knew how to keep secrets safe.

So no, she didn't pass on any memorable quotes, and her towels were not stacked and folded by color in her linen closet. She never said, "In life you're gonna have to do things you don't want

to do. And if you can't get out of them, then get into them."
And she never said, "Be a good listener. Don't judge people." She
didn't have to say those things because she did something far
more powerful. She showed me exactly how it was done.

Prompt

*Try your hand at writing a short essay about any topic of your
choosing.*

CHAPTER 50

Write Everything

I tell everyone in my Writing from the Heart workshops that their story is vital and must be told. What I don't tell them is that not every story is worthy of publication. It's the writing of the story that, to me, is the crucial part.

My father wrote my mother love poems, Ogden Nash kinds of poems. I have a few, and I laminated them for my grandchildren. My grandfather wrote me letters in Yiddish when I was in San Diego, right after I graduated college. There would be a few words in English perfectly spelled, and I knew he had copied them from a card he had probably received himself. There would be "have a wonderful day" right next to one impossible-to-make-out word: *venugonagitmerit*. Translation: "When are you going to get married?" And when my mother was eighty-seven, I gave her a journal so she could record some memories. There are still many stories I'd like to have but don't. I don't have my grandmother's account of what it was like to see the blue tattooed numbers on her brother's arm, knowing he had been a prisoner in Auschwitz. I don't have my mother's reaction to my father's heart attack and her loneliness and fear over how to navigate life with two kids and no money at the young age of forty-four. I don't have my great-grandparents' anything.

Your story didn't start with you, and it won't end with you. You're smack in the middle of it right now. So even if you aren't able to get your story out into the world, imagine what a gift it will be for your future family. Write it for them.

Prompt

What's the most urgent story you want to put on the page?

CHAPTER 51

Quoting People

Rather than misquoting someone (because who can remember exactly what anyone said?), it's best to say something along the lines of, "This is what I remember she said," or, "It went something like this." That way you don't have to use quotation marks all over the place, and you won't get sued by your Aunt Margaret.

Prompt

Quote three people, beginning with: "I remember she [or he] said something like..."

CHAPTER 52

What If My Recollections Are Muddy?

Remember when you were little and you tried to get your mother's attention, and by the time she was ready to listen, you had forgotten what you were going to say? And if she was a harried mom and hadn't taken parenting classes, she might have said, "If it was so important, you would remember it."

Memory plays tricks.

I have been giving this same prompt to my groups forever. It never fails to create intimacy in the sacred circle. The assignment is: "Dinner at our house was …"

Someone once asked me how many times I had written it. Oy. "None," I answered. Actually, I couldn't remember a thing about our dinners. "It always amazes me," I continued, "how many details people write when they do this prompt." I decided I would write "Dinner at our house might have been…" I wrote about linen napkins and white candles and the button under the table that my mother would step on to call the maid. I even named her Shannon. I included my grandfather, who was a jovial judge, and my grandmother, who made the best pies in southern Connecticut, and I wrote and wrote and imagined the perfect dinner, a composite of the best parts from all the dinners I had heard about in my many years of teaching, and all my fantasies about what it would have been like to grow up in a beautiful house with beautiful food. I cherry-picked elegance and ease. And I circled and lied and pretended and created and invented, and little by little, I found myself diving into my real story. The house was cold. The fridge was empty. The table wobbled. The linoleum was chipped. We didn't eat until 9:30, when my parents came home from work. And then I remembered my father taking my mother into his arms and dancing around the kitchen, singing, "She may be weary, women do get weary...Wearing the same shabby dress...And when she's weary, try a little tenderness."

I burst into sobs and dropped tears all over the paper. And that's when I realized that the reason I had been so resistant was I knew how painful it would be to remember. But also how much pain I had been carrying, and how liberating it was to get that stuff out of me and onto the page.

So if you can't remember...need I say more? Try a little tenderness.

And if you really can't remember, let it go. Listen to your mother: if it doesn't come back to you, maybe it wasn't that important.

I ended up writing the story over and over. Here's one of my attempts:

Dinner at Our House

Dinner at our house was at the mahogany dining room table with the three extra leaves stored in the rec room under the antique pool table for Christmas, Thanksgiving, and Easter, when thirty-five of our closest cousins and bestest friends would descend on Mother and Abigail, the head cook and bottle washer, where the aroma of gravy and biscuits and vanilla and cinnamon and turnips and duck a l'orange filled the air like so much culinary perfume. I vowed never to leave this womb of warmth and nourishment.

Oops. That was my roommate Lang's dinner, and if she hadn't had two alcoholic parents, it would have been as ideal as I just described.

No, dinner at our house was at the big farm table, with homemade chicken pot pies, our own chickens, my mother's own pies — always room for guests and farmhands. The oven was always on, even in summer, but the heat never bothered us. There was too much food and laughter to notice.

Oops. That wasn't my dinner either.

OK, OK. Dinner at our house was late, very late, maybe 9:30, at the Formica table with one wobbly leg in our kitchen with the chipped linoleum floor, our parents dragging their exhausted selves into the house after long, long days at their jobs, which they hated, and if they made any money at all it went to the rent on our three-room, five-room, four-room flats with the mean landlords. There was a succession of them.

And the money went to payments for the old Chevy, which broke down periodically with the same regularity as my father's eruptions over the empty bag of Lorna Doones. "Who ate the last cookie?" he would bark.

That was my mother's cue to flee the table with the beginning of her nightly migraine. My sister, who had eaten the first, last, and all the middle cookies, would run from the extra helping of rage she had asked for, and I, at nine and in training to be a mediator for the Middle East, would somehow grab my family from the three corners of disappointment, beg my parents to dance their dance, and watch while he crooned into her ear, "She may be weary, women do get weary... Wearing the same shabby dress... And when she's weary, try a little tenderness." And when he twirled her into the broken chair, I would prod him into telling one of his "do you walk to school or take your lunch" non sequitur jokes, and somehow giggles would transcend the pain and we would hold hands and my mother would get the pineapple upside-down cake she had baked at six that morning and our eyes would fill with the tears of having run the gamut of all the emotions known to humankind. We would collectively plead and vow that tomorrow night would be different, that tomorrow night would be better, that tomorrow night would be easier, though in our bruised and wide-open loving hearts, we knew, just like the Palestinians and the Jews with their ancient tribal warfare, it was probably going to be exactly the same.

Prompt

Write your "Dinner at our house was..."

CHAPTER 53

You Don't Get to Skip the Pain Part

Often I start my writing class by saying, "We're alchemists: We can turn shit into gold. We can take what happened to us — the traumas, the hurts, the tiny murders — and we can transform them into something beautiful. But the most important part of the equation is ... first we have to *feel* it. You can't skip the pain part."

And then when Dan died I woke up with a backache. I joked (because I was numb), "Dan's got my back." A friend gifted me with a drumming/healing workshop in Florida. I flew down, but planes aren't good for six-feet-tall passengers, and when we landed my back was searing. For six days I sat in a stupid position drumming on a stupid pillow, and by the time I got home I was flat on my back. I couldn't move, and the pain was excruciating. I did chiro. I did acupuncture. I lay my head on books doing what I thought was the Alexander Technique. I took Advil. I took Tylenol. I read a book on anger and the back. I even went upside down in one of those contraptions, but the pain didn't let up. And then one morning I suddenly heard my pompous Self speaking: *We're alchemists. We can turn shit into gold. But the most important part of the equation is ... first we have to* feel *it.*

Oh, I thought, *I* have to feel it*? Moi? The teacher has to feel it too?* I started laughing at my ridiculous Self and then started sobbing. And wailing. And pounding on the floor, and two days later my backache was gone, and I began the long process of delayed grieving.

I know we store grief in our bodies. But knowing and living the knowing are two different things. When you're writing your memoir, you must know intellectually that you can't skip the pain part, and you must also know from your experience what you're talking about.

So now when I start the workshop with "We're alchemists, we turn shit into gold..." it's not something I read in a book somewhere; it's my actual gut talking.

My sister died on December 2, 2020. A week later I was googling houses and land for sale in Vermont. I emailed a friend and asked her why she had moved to Quechee, a charming small town a few hours from Boston. She said, "It's filled with a bunch of old hippies. It's as left as left can be, and Nance, for you, there's a club with two huge Olympic-size pools so you can do your laps till the cows come home." And since it was Vermont, I think she meant that literally.

I didn't like the sound of the word *club*. However, she assured me, it wasn't an exclusive kind of thing, and membership was included for anyone who lived in her neighborhood. And she added, "We happen to have two acres on our property we could sell you." I loved the thought of living near my dear friend.

So last month, the first time off the Rock (the island of Martha's Vineyard) in a year, my husband and I drove the three hours up and looked at the land. It was beautiful, and we came home to discuss the matter. Joel said, "Why all of a sudden do you want to go to Vermont?" I said, "I think I need a retreat." "Oh," he said, "Covid and being on lockdown on an island isn't enough of a retreat for you?" I said, "OK, maybe a retreat's not it."

Then I googled houses in Maine. I adore my niece who lives way up north and thought it would be great to live near her. But Joel still works and needs to be within two hours of Boston, so northern Maine was out.

When I told my friend Jane my fantasy plans, her immediate response was, "You're fleeing. Instead of grieving, you're running away." "No," I said, "that's not what this is about."

She instructed, as only a close friend can, "Do not buy anything! Do not go anywhere. Do not make any big decisions until your year of mourning is up."

My husband asked if I was bored. I said no. He asked if I had cabin fever. I said no. He asked if I no longer loved our house. I said I totally loved our house. He said, "So what is it?"

What is it indeed, I thought.

I went for a long walk and asked myself all the same questions.

All I could come up with was, *Maybe I'm looking for a teacher, someone older (is there anyone older?), a mentor. Maybe I'm looking for my spiritual community.*

Someone told me that Taos was filled with healers and teachers so, back to googling. I found some spectacularly interesting dwellings called Earthships. They are completely off the grid, and they are absolutely beautiful.

I had been in Santa Fe a few years back, and I loved the weather, how dry it was, the hot sun in the daytime and the cold, clear air at night. Plus, my favorite part of winter, snowstorms, have become too few and far between here on the Vineyard. And it snowed while we were out there.

I booked a flight to New Mexico. I reserved a car and I rented one of the gorgeous Earthships for a week.

Meanwhile, the husband who does not like flying because of the amount of CO_2 airplanes put into the environment, and who has no desire to own another house, didn't say no. The man sometimes calls me a force of nature, and I think he knows if he had said no I might have pushed against the no rather than making a discerning decision based on facts.

What Jane had said about fleeing kept inserting itself into my compulsive thinking. Two thoughts about my shopping list for Cronigs, one thought about fleeing. Three thoughts about where to find that white balsamic vinegar Suzy uses in her fabulous salad dressing, one thought about fleeing.

In my workshops, after I said the "most important part of the equation is . . . first we have to *feel* it" part, I would add, "If you don't feel it, if you numb out, if you stuff the sorrow, it will find itself somehow in your body. It will marinate in your kidneys or your liver or your heart."

When Dan died, I hadn't taken any of my own advice and had distracted myself with as many activities as I could crowd into a day. It took me about a month of first being diagnosed with atrial fibrillation and then having that awful backache. Like a dream deferred, my willingness to suffer emotionally was delayed, drying up like a raisin in the sun.

In the wake of my sister's death, there I was once more, not listening to my own sage wisdom. I heard myself say, *You can't skip the pain part.* And there I was once again, trying everything in the book to skip the pain part. Buying land in Vermont. Flying off to New Mexico to investigate living a sustainable lifestyle under the pretense that I needed a spiritual community and some kind of teacher. Then it hit me: The teacher is Grief. And I know her. Intimately. And she's right here in my little cabin.

And the spiritual community? That's you.

I canceled the trip.

Prompt

Have you tried to skip the pain part in any of your life's stories? Write one.

CHAPTER 54

Sometimes You Need an Outside
Story to Be the Shift in Consciousness

Many years ago when my mother was in her seventies, I told her that when the time came we could add a room onto our cabin, that she would never be shipped off to a cold, heartless nursing home, that to take care of her would be an honor.

"Sweetheart," she said, "that's very generous and thoughtful of you, but you can't make such a promise. No one knows what the future will bring."

I said, "I do. I'm going to drive you to your bridge games. I'm going to make homemade soup for you. I'm going to wash and comb your hair. We're going to do watercolors. We're gonna watch *Jeopardy*."

Although my plan was elaborate and imaginative and definitely genuine, it was not rooted in reality. The game I played gave her a sense of security and me a sense of what a good person I was.

But Rude Awakening met with Happily Ever After. When my mother came to visit she announced that she was seriously thinking of accepting our offer and asked if we could talk about it. She had brought an article titled "How to Best Live with an Aging Parent." All the issues were covered: what to do about money, how to contact people in the community for other support services, how to keep healthy boundaries in intimate relationships, how to handle the kitchen duties, the refrigerator, the food supplies, everything from Ensure to insurance.

Her first morning with us she called me into my tiny office, which doubles as a guest room, and said, "Honey, can you figure out this radio? I can't seem to get it to work."

"Sure, sweet one," I said. I got my glasses so I could see the small numbers, sat down, and set her alarm. Just as I was leaving, she said, "Honey, did you already make coffee because I would love a cup right now."

"Not yet," I said, "but I'm on it." As I was waiting for the water to boil, I hauled her bag up on the bed, and together we started making room in the closet — granted, stuff I should have done before her arrival. I switched all the things she might need that were on shelves too high for her to reach and too low for her to crouch.

Just as I was about to run out the door because I was late for work, she said, "Sweetheart, do you have a small dish for my vitamins? I have to lay them out at night so I'll know which ones I took and which are still sitting there when I go to bed." I didn't have a small dish but I found a little pinch pot one of the kids made in third grade that I use for tea bags, and she said it was perfect. Then she wanted me to help her make the bed (she never leaves her bed unmade), give her something good to read (she had just finished her book), and show her where the garlic and the lemons were because it looked as if the avocados were just ripe enough (in case she decided to make guacamole and I hadn't yet returned).

I was distracted as I drove down the road. I kept thinking of how hard it had been just to leave the house that morning. None of the small things she had asked for were any big deal. Nothing required major work or even major concentration. It was just that I was used to my morning solitude and my morning ritual. I felt ashamed that I had the tiniest flicker of annoyance that my big-deal morning routine had been disturbed. Was it the coffee or the dish or the radio that was such a hardship? I lectured my selfish self. I promised to do better. I mean, I love this woman and I love being with her, hanging with her, living with her. Wasn't that why I had invited her to come?

That night before I went to sleep, I read the article. I tossed and turned and saw the sunrise.

This is nothing, I thought. *Wait till she really needs me.* I thought about my friend Mary, whose father moved in with her after her mother died, how disruptive and demanding and even violent he had become. I thought about my friend Paul, whose mother had moved in with him and his wife and three small children. At best she had been a negative woman. Now in her later years, she was impossible. I remember my own grandmother, who had lived with us at ninety, wandering into the street in the middle of the night, my mother chasing after her, my parents arguing early in the morning. She was my father's mother, and my mother loved her. "I can't put her in a nursing home. I won't," she had cried.

My mom had always been joyous, delicious to be with, and a wonderful sport. But that was then, and this is now. Living in a strange new place, would she lose some of her independence? Would she miss her friends and need me more? Would she be disoriented and think my bathroom was her bathroom? Would she have her own telephone line? Would she be included in all our evenings, or would she sit alone, straining to hear the laughter and the tinkling of glasses?

My mother's life had just begun so many transitions. One of her friends had gotten sick. Another had died. My mom had to change dentists twice. One retired and one expired. Same thing with her doctors. It seemed as if her infrastructure was crumbling, and rebuilding wasn't even an option.

The threat that she could deteriorate was looming, and here I was complaining about a few interruptions. I decided to take a walk in the woods. As I walked, I remembered a story I had heard many years earlier.

There was a young Chinese farmer. He worked hard in his fields all day. He had many children to feed and a wife who was not well. One day he looked up from his toil and saw his old father sitting and rocking on the porch. *He doesn't work,* he thought. *He doesn't help. All he does is eat and sleep. He costs me too much time and money. I will have to get rid of him.* And so the young man went about making a box. When he was finished, he put the box on his wheelbarrow and walked up to the house. "Father," he said, "I can't afford you anymore. Get in." The old man climbed into the box. The farmer covered and sealed the box and clumsily wheeled it up to the top of the mountain, where he planned to send the old man plummeting. As they were bumping along, the father suddenly began banging violently on the ceiling of the box. "What is it, Father?" the man said with exasperation. The old man's muffled voice said, "I understand what you are doing. I know how hard times are. But save the box. Your son will need it."

I have never run the fifty-yard dash. I have never had to rush from danger or toward safety. But I flew back to my house as if my life depended on it.

Whatever had I been thinking? Whatever was I planning to do with this time I had started to resent giving to my mother? What could be more important than serving her in her last years? Was I willing to let her die, and in my grief and longing, wish I could get her coffee?

This was a gift. I hadn't even recognized it as such.

I burst into my house, took one look at my mother, grabbed her, hugged her, and said, "First we're gonna take a drive to see the sunset, then we're getting lobsters, then we are coming home and designing the addition for your very own room."

Prompt

Write a story in which the main character changes her mind.

CHAPTER 55

Writing to Heal

Sometimes, at the end of my workshop, I'll say, "I should really call this workshop Writing to Heal, but then no one would come." We all chuckle. Because the truth is most people know what healing will entail. Digging deep and feeling pain. Who signs up for that? So Writing from the Heart (a much more benign title for a writing seminar) is my sneaky way of getting you to go deep, feel pain and, yes, have major healing.

I have a million stories about how writing your sorrow is healing. I have had the privilege of witnessing personal transformation in writers who have been holding on to their pain for dear life and then after writing, find brand-new, healthier ways to look at what happened to them.

When people ask me (and they often do) if the workshop is therapy, my answer is, "No, it's not therapy. It's *therapeutic* to write your story with the support of nonjudgmental listeners," which leads me to ...

Storytelling in the Medical World

Rita Charon, a medical doctor, started a major at Columbia University called narrative medicine. Basically, it is about physicians paying exquisite attention to patients' stories and using those stories for healing. Doctors listening to their patients' narratives create higher levels of empathy, which translates into more positive outcomes.

I got to be a presenter at a workshop led by this brilliant woman, and it validated what intuitively I must have already known. In my Writing from the Heart workshops, I have one rule, and that is when you finish reading, we will tell you what we loved. That's it. I make it very clear that the workshop is not about publishing or editing or showing the writer how they can improve. In fact, I joke at the beginning of the first session, "I don't teach writing, I teach gushing." So when people finish reading their very personal pieces and get the feedback I model (which is usually filled with repeating back to them some of their greatest lines and a few *holy shit, you're amazing*s), I have seen people lose years of worry from their faces. They look radiant, they sit up straighter, and the next time they write, their voices are louder.

One exercise we did at that workshop involved thirty-six people sitting in a circle. We had three minutes to tell any story of our choice to the person sitting next to us. Since we knew what the exercise was designed to produce, we told our most difficult stories. After we had all shared and been listened to, the leader rang a bell and we went around the circle and told our partner's story as if it were our own. The effect of repeating what we had just heard, not as if it were some random thing from out there but rather one from inside our own hearts and guts, was powerful and shockingly painful.

Narrative medicine is now being taught at some medical schools, and doctors are finally getting to be the healers they probably dreamed of being when they applied to med school in the first place.

Prompt

Experiment with a writing partner. Do the sharing exercise. Then write their story as if it were your own.

CHAPTER 56

Read Your Stuff Out Loud

After you've taken a break, and you're reading over what you have eked out, read it out loud. Read it out loud so you'll know when you've used the word *purple* and it's too guttural and you need something softer, like *lavender*. Read it out loud so you can catch when you have written the word *rug* three times in a row. Repeating a word or a phrase is understandable when you're on your first draft. After all, it was a rug, but now that you're working it, it's also a carpet, a dhurrie, or a Berber.

Repetition when it's intentional can be powerful. Repetition when it's lazy is a yawn in the making. You can have the best sentence or word combo in the world, but if you throw it in again, you have just diluted all its power.

That's another reason why you have to take a break and put your writing aside. When you go back to it you can see it with fresh eyes while still wearing your editor's cap.

Prompt

Read your most recent entry out loud. Listen for music. Make changes in details, in color.

CHAPTER 57

You Don't Need a Writing Studio to Write Your Memoir

Many years ago during one of my Writing from the Heart workshops, one of the participants experienced a major life transformation. The next year she invited Joel and me for dinner. At dessert, she toasted me and said, "I have a surprise for you. It's actually my thank-you for helping me heal and find my voice." She led us down a lovely winding path with twinkly fairy lights, and we came upon an opening and a sweet wooden building, with a stained-glass window and high ceilings. She opened the door with a flourish and announced, "This is my writing studio. Because of *you*." On the desk was a brand-new computer, a vase filled with light-peach tea roses (how did she know my favorite color of rose?), and a Herman Miller Aeron chair, waiting for her highness to sit and write her *New York Times* bestseller. On the way home I was so envious I practically threw up the chocolate pistachio mousse tower her cook had spent the day preparing.

She had a surprise for me? I bellowed in the car. *The most gorgeous little studio anyone has ever seen, she had built because of me? While I'm sitting in our cramped living room with my MacBook Pro on my lap? No wonder I can't write.*

And my wise husband said, "What a bunch of bullshit. If you want to write, you can write anywhere. And you know this. You wrote one of the best things I've ever read while you were sitting on the floor, folding laundry with two kids crawling all over you."

You don't need a studio to write. If you think that, know that's just your lame excuse for not doing what you keep saying you want to do.

So let me say it again: *You don't need a studio to write.* Just your desire and your discipline.

Prompt

Make a list of three things you thought you needed that you actually don't need to start writing.

CHAPTER 58

You Can Write Like This?
About Stuff Like This?

The first time I read J.D. Salinger was the first time I knew I could write. Holden Caulfield was a kid and spoke like a kid. He used regular words like *phonies*, and the constant expression *and all* gave him a human quality I hadn't found yet in anything I had read in school. He sounded like a real person, someone who could be sitting next to me in algebra. He wrote about feelings and alienation and God. Until Salinger, I thought writers had to sound like this: "Why so pale and wan fond lover? Prithee why so pale? Will, when looking well can't move her, Looking ill prevail?"

He gave me permission to sound like me. I was fifteen, and my father had just died. I started writing very bad poetry without feeling self-conscious about whether or not it was "good." What a gift to be able to express my broken heart and not worry about whether I sounded educated enough, or whether I sounded like a real writer *and all* and still be able to get so much of my pain and confusion onto the page. What a gift to be able to be ambivalent about God and organized religion and not feel guilty.

I hereby give you my permission and my blessing, and my unfolded laundry.

Prompt

Has someone given you permission to sound like you? Write about how that changed your writing.

CHAPTER 59

Too Many Crises Are Gonna Be Too Hard to Swallow

The other night I was with two girlfriends, telling them about my sordid past. They knew most of it because we've been good friends for years, but I was adding to the long list of childhood horror shows that I felt I had endured. At some point I saw them glaze over. But I kept going, being the storyteller steamroller that I am.

Later that night when I was alone, going over the monologue that I had somehow felt I needed to perform, I realized that even though all of what I had told them had actually happened, it was too much. They didn't need to hear every graphic detail. They had gotten my history years before. They knew who I was. They knew my playlist, and all I did was gild the poor wilting lily, almost rendering all the other stuff unbelievable.

Pick and choose. *Choose the best stories, and omit the ones that illustrate the same point.* We don't need to hear how much you suffered. We need to know how you survived. Banging your reader over the head with too many tragedies only gives them a migraine and a reason to write a bad review on Amazon, or worse, return your book to the library unread.

Prompt

Make a list of some personal crises. Now choose the big one and eliminate the rest. Write about the big one.

Humor

Humor is funny. It's not mean. If it's mean, it's not humor. I have heard barbs accompanied with the one-line justification "I was just kidding." Oh, you kidder, you. Don't try to sneak in your resentment with sarcasm. There's a place for sarcasm. Just cop to it.

Prompt

Write a snarky piece. Then see if you can remove the snark and make the piece funny.

CHAPTER 61

Great Writing without Going Anywhere

You have just written the best paragraph you have ever penned. Every word is gorgeous. You are bursting with pride at your brilliance. You read it over and over, prouder every time. After you come down from your lofty Pulitzer Prize–winning acceptance speech, you read it again and realize it doesn't add anything to the scene you're building. It's just beautiful writing. Now you work to get it into the narrative. Somewhere. Anywhere. You don't care that it doesn't add anything where you're trying to put it, and you work and you insert and you delete and you weave and you plop it like bird poo from the sky.

This will be the hardest thing: you must admit it doesn't fit.

Prompt

Look through your pages and see if there's something that doesn't fit. Then put it in a file with your dead darlings. Or, if you don't already have a file of dead darlings, let this be the beginning of one. (They're not really dead. They're resting and waiting for you to revive them at the proper time.)

CHAPTER 62

Rewriting Is
Actually Where You Start

It's harder to make bad writing good than good writing better.

— RICHELLE E. GOODRICH

For years all my writer friends talked about how the rewriting process is their favorite part of writing. Not so with me. I hate going back over what I've written. I find it tedious. I have to drag myself to the computer and make myself pretend it's the first time I'm reading. It doesn't always work, and half the time I give up. I attribute this quality to my laziness. But I do know that when I actually get down to business, the rewrite is a thousand times better.

And how do I know that?

Once I lost eighty-six pages of what was to be my memoir. Usually I just write and then fix. But this particular time, I actually had been editing as I went along. I was very pleased with the results and the meticulous way I was working. And then, since I'm a Luddite, and autocorrect and all its relatives have it in for me, the document disappeared. I brought my computer down to the business center, and they couldn't find the document. My husband bought the tool to remove the hard drive and brought it to the best data-recovery company in Boston. They told him they work for the police departments and almost never fail. There would be no charge if they couldn't retrieve it; they were that confident. They asked for key words. I had whole key sentences. They couldn't find it.

I walked around dazed for a few days and took it as a sign that

I wasn't supposed to write a memoir. And I didn't write anything for quite some time after that. Finally, I began to miss the act of writing and decided that maybe the timing was right to start again. This time my consciousness was different, my discipline was better, and my writing was much clearer. It was a rewrite of sorts. But time had provided me with a kind of newness.

We don't always have the luxury of time, so rewriting is a good habit to get into. If you manage it, let me know how you did it.

This is one of those *do as I say, not as I do* deals.

Prompt

Write a quick piece. No thinking. No editing. No revising. "The last time I saw him ..." Now rewrite it. Take your time.

CHAPTER 63

We've All Heard the Writing Advice
Show, Don't Tell

But when I heard it years ago I didn't really know what it meant. I felt like telling *was* showing.

Here's a *telling* example:

Out of the blue my mother would sometimes fly into rages. My little sister and I were scared of her, especially at night when she came home from work. But there were other times when she was nice.

Here it is *showing*:

At 5:45 every weekday night my little sister and I would kneel on the couch in the living room, waiting for my mother's car headlights to shine into the window. The second they hit, we would run up the stairs as fast as our little ten- and six-year-old legs could carry us. We'd slam our bedroom door and hide in the closet. We could tell by the way her feet sounded whether we were in for a tirade or a song.

Prompt
Write a tell version, and then write the show version.

CHAPTER 64

The Stories We Tell Ourselves about Ourselves

Many years ago, I attended a Power of Awareness workshop with Jack Kornfield, the Buddhist meditation teacher. On the second day, he talked about "the stories we tell ourselves about ourselves," the stories that no longer serve us. The next morning I took a walk around the campus. There was a dusting of snow and I slipped and fell. As I was hobbling back to the main building, I thought, *Well, of course I fell. I have weak ankles.* And my next thought was, *Wait a minute. I don't have weak ankles. My sister has weak ankles.* I adored my older sister and absorbed every quality I could about her. Including her deficiencies. How long, I wondered, had I been living with the illusion that I had weak ankles? I realized I had never learned to skate! I had actually used the weak-ankle excuse and never enjoyed a winter sport for absolutely no reason. Talk about a story I told myself about myself. How many more of these did I have? How many do you have?

I came home from that workshop and hired an eleven-year-old friend of mine to teach me to skate at the indoor rink on the Vineyard. I can't say I'll be in the Olympics anytime soon, but I know how to skate holding someone's hand, and I will never again say I have weak ankles.

Maybe you had a music teacher tell you to "mouth the words" because he said you were tone-deaf. And that took care of your joy of singing. Maybe your artist aunt told you that you had no sense of color because at the ripe old age of six, you used only black and brown. And that ended any artistic aspirations you might have entertained. Check the stories you're telling yourself!

Prompt

What story do you tell yourself that no longer serves?

CHAPTER 65

How about Serializing
Your Memoir in a Blog?

Blogs are big. Anyone can have a blog. They're as easy as rolling off a log, to quote James Taylor, quoting a *Merrie Melodies* cartoon. And if you get a following, you might even catch the attention of a publisher so that the blog can turn into the book.

One of the advantages of writing a blog is that you will want to write every day. And it won't be scary because no one is pressuring you. And your entries can be as short as you like. So consider blogging instead of slogging.

Prompt
Write three titles for your blog.

CHAPTER 66

Go to the Top

People in charge who have "made it" probably made it because they didn't play by the rules. Worker bees can't make decisions, so if you send your manuscript or your article or your poem to someone at the bottom they may love it but not be able to send it upstairs to the boss. It will languish in a pile on a desk filled with other rejects. Find the top person and write to him. Call her. Email him. Bug them. Show up at their coffee place. Beg. Make the personal connection. The squeaky wheel can be annoying, but the squeak is louder than silence.

I used to be a closet writer fantasizing that I would one day get something published. Each month I would read *Lear's* cover to cover, imagining my story inside those pages. Finally I got up my nerve and looked at the masthead to decide whom, among the many editors, I should address my submission to. I landed on a name that kind of jumped out at me. She felt somehow familiar and safe. Two weeks later I received a phone call (those were the days when people actually talked to each other). The woman on the other end of the line was laughing. She said, "This is Linda Gutstein from *Lear's*. I love your story. We're going to buy it, but can I ask you a question?" I was so shocked and thrilled, but I had the wherewithal to say, "Sure, ask away." And she said, "Why did you send it to me? I'm not the features editor." And I said, "Your name was Jewish and had the word *guts* in it." She laughed even harder and told me she wasn't actually Jewish, but that began my journey with a major New York magazine. It may have been igno-rance or innocence, but I had gone to the top and was rewarded twenty-fold.

And today, as I was writing this, I received an email (now you hear from editors by email, but it's just as exciting) that the top editor of *Moment* magazine has bought this story of mine:

In my junior year of high school, my principal called me into his office and asked me where I wanted to go to school. When I told him Duke, he asked me why. I told him I heard it was the Yale of the South, and Yale doesn't take girls.

The year was 1958. He said, "What about the University of Virginia? They have a great theater department." I said, "Yeah, but I don't want to go that far south." Dr. Rives leaned over, opened a drawer, and pulled out an atlas. "Here," he said. "Look, here's North Carolina and here's Virginia." He could have said, "You have no business going to college if you don't even know the map of the United States." But he didn't. Instead he said, "Send away for a UVA catalog. You'll love it there."

On the very first page there was a black-and-white photograph of the Daisy Chain. Seven blonde girls, with perfect pageboy hairdos, organdy gowns, and white gloves sitting in a semicircle surrounded by a field of daisies. My immediate reaction was *I have to go there. If I go there I will become a gentile.* And that, more than any education, was my goal.

I had had it with being Jewish. My parents had tried to assimilate, but it wasn't enough for me. Jews couldn't have Christmas. I had had Christmas envy from birth. Jews couldn't be cheerleaders, Jews couldn't go to the cotillion, Jews couldn't belong to the only country club. The biggest compliment I could get was, "You don't look Jewish."

Those blonde beauties were my ticket.

The next page had photographs of the ring dance. Marines in full dress uniform, from Quantico, down the road, were the escorts, and once again the girls were picture-perfect, feminine, and beautiful. I was six feet tall and weighed in at 195. My hair was dirt-brown and frizzed when the dew point was up. I would go to the University of Virginia, and Eliza Doolittle would have nothing on me.

My mother, who had been widowed only three years earlier and hadn't found her power yet, had never driven on a highway. So there I was that September, in seat 11B on a Greyhound bus from Hartford, Connecticut, to Fredericksburg, Virginia, to begin my freshman year at Mary Washington College of the University of Virginia. For nine hours and one changeover, I clutched my small suitcase, which held three cotton shirtwaist dresses with the traditional rope belt, one pair of sneakers, a cardigan sweater with pearl buttons that my mother had put on layaway, my Ban deodorant, a bar of Ivory soap, and a box of Kotex. I hadn't read the what-to-bring section thoroughly, so I didn't know we were supposed to bring our own towels. And sheets. I didn't pack a great pillow because I hadn't yet learned what a great pillow felt like.

Growing up in Connecticut, I had never traveled farther than New Jersey. I was not prepared for what the South would be like. When I got off the bus, I looked for the ladies' room and saw that there were two. One marked Ladies and the other Colored. I remember standing outside the two doors not quite knowing what to do. There was no way I was going to buy into this backward prejudiced small-town thinking. I was a Northerner. I had friends who were Black. What was this?

If I went into the one that said Colored, how would people feel? Relieved or invaded? Finally, because my convictions of being an ally of the underdog were so strong, I tentatively walked into the one that said Colored. If there had been an audience yelling "Door number one! Door number one!" that would have helped. But there was no audience. And as it turned out, as I could tell from the looks on the faces of the few folks standing around, that wasn't the correct choice.

But nothing could dampen my spirit. The campus was magnificent: weeping willows, little bridges over trickling streams, brick buildings with white columns that told me Thomas Jefferson had slept here.

On the second night, a bunch of us were gathered in one of the blonde pageboy girls' rooms. There were about nine of us, and everyone was telling stories and jokes and laughing. I was in heaven. Then someone told an anti-Semitic joke. Everyone laughed... *including me.*

I spent the next two days having a right brain–left brain argument with myself.

What am I doing here?

I should have gone to Cornell.

But you are here.

Think of yourself as a cultural-exchange student.

Maybe I just won't tell.

Oh, and you're gonna keep your secret for four years?

If I tell them I'm Jewish, I won't have any friends.

You came here to not be Jewish, didn't you?

And on and on I nattered.

On the fifth night, I found myself in the same room with the same girls, listening to the same stories and brand new anti-Semitic jokes. And suddenly I raised my hand, and then I called on myself. I proceeded to tell a Jewish joke with a perfect Yiddish accent. Every blonde pageboy roared with laughter, and as the giggles died down, I raised my hand again and I said, "I am a Jewish person. I am the only one who can tell these jokes."

The silence was excruciatingly loud. And then one of the adorable pageboys said, "O Naincy, I cain't believe you're a Jew. You're just so darlin'!" And another one said, "Ah have got to bring you home to meet my Daiddy. He's not gonna believe I met a Jew!"

Now, I knew in my heart that both of these were compliments, even though they sounded brutal. But it was the third one that threw me. She asked if she could touch my "hayah." She was clearly looking for horns. I wish I had known then what I found out years later. Moses, it turns out, was depicted by Michelangelo with two horns on his head. The Hebrew word for *horn* is close to the Hebrew word for *beams of light.*

I let her touch my hayah, and as soon the laughter and the joy resumed, something shifted in me and I knew I had to stay.

For part of my tuition, I worked in the dining hall. All the kitchen help were Black men. And all us scholarship girls were the waitresses. Once we had served everyone, we could go out into the dining room and eat at a special table reserved for the help. I usually chose to stay back and eat with the guys who were becoming my buds. We would sing the songs my sister and I used to listen to late at night on the one Black radio station out of Buffalo, New York.

One day in the middle of my solo, which I was singing at the top of my lungs, pretending to be one of the Platters, "Oh-oh-oh yes, I'm the Great Pretender," Mrs. McGinnis, my boss, came barreling out of her office yelling, "Naincy, I know you are from up nohth, but evrah tahm you bring them nigres up, I got to bring 'em back down. Now, if you want to keep this job, you got to go out front and eat with your people." I knew what she meant. My people were white people. But the guys I was working with were my people.

Mrs. McGinnis caught me a few more times and I worried that I would lose my job, so I stopped hanging out with my sweet new friends and started "behaving."

One day one of the guys came up to me, waving tickets in his hand. "Naincy, you like Jimmy Reed?" I said yes, even though I didn't know who Jimmy Reed was. He handed me four tickets that read "Friday night at the armoury!" I got three other Yankees to say yes, and we ordered a taxi to take us off campus.

We were right on time, but not a soul was inside except for the three white policemen who greeted us with "Y'all from up the colich?" "Yes," I answered. "Well," one of the central casting cops said, "This here is the nigre armoury."

"We have tickets," I snapped and handed them over.

Nancy Wilson blared over the loudspeakers, and empty seats lined all four walls. One of the pasty-faced policemen came over to me, gesturing with his chin at the fat cop in the corner. "Sarg wants to know how much you weigh." Without thinking I gave a wiseass answer: "Tell him he can't count that high." Little did I know, that would be my undoing.

We had a Friday night curfew of 10:00, and it was 9:27 when all my guys walked in. When they saw me they went wild. "Lookee here! Lookee here! Naincy, our Naincy is here!" "The Twist" was playing. *Let's twist again like we did last summer.* I jumped up and danced with them all.

We made it back into the dorm just as the headmistress was locking the door. There was a phone call for me. "Hah, Naincy. This is Mary Beth Lawla. You are required to appear at Dean Harwood's home tomorruh at three p.m." *Required.* "Can you tell me what this is about?" I asked. Her answer was chilling. "Ah think you know."

I hung up and called my mother. I said, "I think I'm going to get thrown out of school tomorrow. But don't worry, because if I do I'll be on the cover of *Life.*" I didn't feel as glib as I sounded.

The next day I was seated on the couch in the middle of a semicircle of seven deans and the president of the University of Virginia. I was shaking. Dean Hargrove spoke first. "The entire community is shocked," she said. "Even the nigres are shocked." Then Dean Honeywell spoke. "Naincy," she said, in all earnest, "would you dance with a maintenance man?" I cleared my throat that didn't need clearing and said, "I have been to three mixers here. All the boys I met were drunk and rude. The boys I danced with Friday night were respectful and polite. I work with them. I know them. They're my friends."

Then the dean of social activities pulled a dainty flowered handkerchief from the cleavage of her ample bosom and said in her smoker's low-throated voice, "Mah only complaint, Naincy, is that you would have gone to a social event [and as if the vapors had finally gotten to her, with hankie in hand she fanned herself] unescorted!"

I wish I had known that one day this could have made a great *Saturday Night Live* bit, but in that moment in 1959, sitting in an inquisition, waiting to hear my fate with absolutely no intention of going to *Life* magazine (what was I thinking?), I just sat and held back the tears.

Finally, they asked if I had anything to say. Barely able to find any volume, I spoke. "I know, 'when in Rome,'" I said, "but I grew up with Negroes, and they're just people with darker skin. They are just like us. Some are good and some are bad. The guys I work with are good. I don't think I should be punished, because I don't think I did anything wrong."

The president of the school never said a word. But the Big Dean, the dean of the whole college, said, "Naincy, we're not going to throw you out. We don't want this kind of publicity. Howevuh, we will be watching you."

"We will be watching you" became my rallying cry. Once I knew I was Teflon before anyone knew what Teflon was, my inner rebel, who obviously had been under the influence of an elephant tranquilizer, woke up. And I started my own mini civil rights movement.

A month before graduation, I played Flora in Tennessee Williams's *27 Wagons Full of Cotton*, and in the middle of a sexy scene the swing we were seated on broke. Splayed on the floor, wearing a satin Victoria's Secret kind of slip, I went into a riff, a monologue about hypocrisy and the War between the States (as the Southerners called it) and the slave block they still had in the center of town. I said, "When I first saw it I wanted to throw red paint all over it. Who's up for a little trip to William Street this Friday night? We'll call it Shabbat Tikkun Olam." Tennessee would have been proud as I instigated my one-woman protest right there center stage.

My mom, who had never left Connecticut, courageously drove with my ninety-two-year-old grandfather the six and a half hours to see me graduate. I introduced her to my friends, the daughters of the Daughters of the American Revolution, and I dragged her to meet my favorite dean, Dean Alvey, who charmed her with his drawl and compliments on what a great job she had done bringing me up.

Walking down the aisle, seeing my precious family, looking forward to flipping that tassel to the other side, I made myself memorize every detail of what I somehow knew I'd need for future reference.

"What happened up there?" my mom asked after the ceremony. "It seemed there was a perfect rhythm. Every girl stepped up on the platform, received her diploma, shook hands with three official-looking old people, and moved off and down the other side. But when you got up there, the rhythm broke. The dean you introduced me to, Dean Alvey, said something to you and they all broke up laughing. What did he say?"

I said, "Oh, this was a riot, Mom. He said, 'Naincy, now that you're leavin' us, the earth is finally gonna settle.' And you're right, they all chuckled."

The joke was on them, though. Virginia was right on the cusp of the sixties. When pot and cocaine and legal abortion and civil rights exploded onto the scene, they probably yearned for my return.

But staying all four years was the best thing I could have done. Running away would have kept me in the closet as a Jew. Instead, I left more Jewish than when I arrived, with my fantasy of becoming someone else put to rest, leaving behind a bunch of Southern belles using Yiddish expressions sprinkled in their everyday conversations — *Now that was a greps, I'm shvitizing, He's a schnorer, Oh, this old schmatta* — and taking with me a BA in English that would get me my first job, teaching high school in San Diego.

I had made peace with my dirt-brown curls, and I had planted and begun watering the seeds of my activism. I knew that the next time someone thought they were paying me a compliment by saying, "You don't look Jewish," I would belt out the beginning of my Haftorah and say, "Oh, but I am. I am so, so very, very Jewish."

Prompt

Submit something today to the top editor of a magazine or blog or any platform you admire and read regularly. Once you have secured an editor, you are allowed to fight for what you want.

CHAPTER 67

Fighting for What You Want

Writing is a business. It's no different from any other business. Bottom line is the first consideration. Pick your fights. You need to let go of some battles and fight the ones that make your work *yours*.

Here's an example of fighting for what you want — and failing. In the early 1980s, when I had a column in *McCall's*, I wrote the following piece and learned the painful lesson about the magazine business: that image was more important than message. Look for the word *luckily*.

Looking Out, Looking In

The question of curtains can divide an almost perfectly harmonious marriage. I don't like curtains; I like seeing what is outside: trees and sky and the occasional human. It's like God's art...framed. But recently we had some remodeling done in our kitchen, and my husband walked in and saw two naked windows.

He said, "We need to cover these immediately."

I said, "Why? Look how pretty the landscape is, and in the morning you see the sun shining and at night you see the moon glowing."

"Please go buy curtains," he said. "The whole world can see us in here."

"What whole world?" I said. "There is one lone neighbor who could possibly see if he climbs up on his roof and bends himself into an L, and then he might get a glimpse of our microwave."

"Don't be funny," my husband said. "He has friends who come over all the time, and they could look straight into these windows."

"With great effort," I said, "and if that's how they want to spend their time, what are they gonna do — watch us tossing our Caesar salad?"

He did not laugh, and since the man asks for little else, I felt I should honor such a small request. So I went shopping for shades. I found out fast enough they're not called shades. They're called *window treatments*. I hated them all. The shades were ugly, and the curtains were worse.

I began researching how my friends have solved the privacy problem. And what did I learn? Several people must be barely tolerating me, decorator-wise. I was shocked at the amount of matching fabric per chair per couch per friend I have. I am still tacking faded antique lace tablecloths to moldings and calling them family heirloom room dividers. Considering that I still have a residue of *House Beautiful* taste left over from my hippie days, we're lucky I didn't try dangling dried and dyed, strung and hung gourd seeds as "window treatments."

"Whatcha get?" my husband asked as soon as he walked in the door.

"Nothing," I told him. "Why can't we leave it stark and simple?"

"Because I want something blocking the view," he insisted. So, reluctantly, I went back in search of the perfect compromise. I settled on yards and yards and yards of white gossamer cheesecloth. The lady at the counter told me cheesecloth was primarily used for cooking turkeys. I thought it best not to go into my marital problems and left with my bundle of gauze.

When I got home, I draped the folds of delicate gossamer fabric over a wooden rod, stepped back to admire my creation — and then my husband came into the kitchen and roared: "What is this? The stuff is totally see-through!"

"Why are you having such a problem?" I moaned.

"Because," he said, "you didn't buy curtains, you bought bandages."

What is this really about? I wondered. My shrink would say it wasn't about window treatments, it was about boundaries. Of course, after giving it two minutes of honest thought I knew that's exactly what it was.

My husband has always been a very private person. He grew up with healthy boundaries. I grew up with none. I thought boundaries were borders on maps, like Australia was yellow and New Zealand was baby-blue. I thought Frost's "good fences make good neighbors" was advice about landscaping. Crossing boundaries, for all I knew, meant stretching the imagination.

I remember when my sons were young, it was all I could do to keep from eavesdropping when their friends would visit. Then, when they were a little older, it was hard to keep myself from going through their corduroy pants pockets and reading their opened and folded-again love notes. And I know I didn't use restraint when girls first started calling them on the phone. I would interrogate them: "So what did she say — and what did you say — and then what did you say?" Luckily, my husband would yell from the other room, "You don't have to give her any answers, guys."

Of course, he was quite right. I had always been too open, too accessible, too pushy, too public, a veritable naked window, if you will. But after a few years of therapy, I learned, among other things, that boundaries define where one *person* ends and another begins.

So now I was having my own little Personal-Growth Test. I looked at my bandaged windows and thought of my damaged childhood, and I said, "What about shutters that open and close?" He smiled, gave me a big hug, and thanked me for understanding. I smiled back and said, "And think of it. At the very least, I won't have to buy cheesecloth for our next twenty, thirty, maybe forty Thanksgivings."

Notice the line "Luckily, my husband would yell from the other room, 'You don't have to give her any answers, guys.'" Well, when *McCall's* sent me the galleys I saw that they had taken out the word *luckily*! You may notice how that changes the meaning. I took a train into New York and sat in a meeting called at my insistence. The room was so crowded I had to sit on the floor. I said "the implication when you take out the word *luckily* is that the man, the husband, the boss is the final word with the children. If you keep *luckily* it implies that we are a team, that I recognize when I'm the asshole, and thank God I married a partner who can save the day, which also implies that he feels the same way. A team. A couple. Not man over woman." I said, "Is this the message you want to be sending to your 17 million readers?" I turned to the big editor and I said, "Remember when you hired me you said you wanted my voice? Please use it!" They all agreed, and when the piece came out in *McCall's* they had left out the word *luckily*. When I called screaming into the phone, they said there was no room in the column inch.

Prompt

Write a piece about fighting for something you did not want to compromise on.

CHAPTER 68

Conclusions on Their Way to Endings

We move into my in-laws' house in Concord and drive the ninety minutes to Spaulding Rehab Hospital in Salem, every day. We arrive at ten in the morning, and we leave at eleven at night. We do this for twelve weeks.

It's December and the neighborhoods remind me of Hartford, where I grew up. Two-family houses close together, slanted aging porches, and old-fashioned multicolored Christmas lights. The warm glow on the snow is comforting. But we could not be in more pain.

We rent books on tape for our return rides to Concord. We like the Philip Roth novels because he reads them himself and his voice is soothing. In the mornings, though, we mostly travel in silence. We are in our own thoughts, our own sadness.

For the past two weeks, Dan hasn't acknowledged us. He stares up at the ceiling, a look of horror on his face. Sometimes his eyes are open; sometimes his lips move. I have asked him, "Dan, is there something you're seeing or hearing that is frightening you?" He doesn't respond.

Friends have been coming occasionally. People who haven't seen Dan for a while can't hide their shock. He's thin and has dark circles under his eyes, and now with the trach and the tubes everywhere, he looks like a handsome young patient on *Grey's Anatomy*. They talk to him in upbeat voices and get the same thing: nothing.

Dan hasn't moved in weeks. The physical therapists who were so enthusiastic in the beginning have stopped scheduling sessions. Every so often they poke their heads in and with their eyes, ask, "What do you think?" and with our heads we say, "No, not today."

My dearest friend, Lorie, comes up from the Vineyard to hang out one Sunday and take me to lunch. I tell Joel to stay home that day; he needs a break. I spend the morning reading to Dan, though there is no reaction. Lorie arrives and sits on the bed and talks to Dan. "Let's go," I say. "I have to get out of here."

We drive to a place where Joel and I have been eating, and we sit and I pick at my food. Lorie tells me there's a show at the Peabody Essex. I am desperate to do anything but go back into that room. So we park near the museum and walk in. The exhibit is a high-fashion costume show. In the first room are eight black mannequins lined up on a platform, wearing everything from the white go-go boots and leather miniskirts of the '60s to a salmon-colored crepe beaded fringe dress from the '20s. I am grateful no one else is around. I can't move. I just stand there sobbing.

Lorie takes my hand and we drive back to Spaulding in total silence. There is nothing she can say. She knows it and I know it, so the silence between us is a gift. Just before I get out of the car, though, she says, "It's so sad, Nance, it's just so sad." And I say, "Yeah, it is sad."

We hug and I walk toward the main building. And then a thought comes into my head. *Yes, of course it is sad. But what else is it? I'm going in there to find out.*

As I'm walking in I'm thinking about the clock that Ram Dass describes in his book *Grist for the Mill*: It's six o'clock and something bad happens, you break your leg. But then it's 6:15 and the surgeon operating is adorable and he's flirting. Then it's 6:25 and you heard he's married, and then its 6:40 and you find out actually he's a widower. And now it's 6:45 and you start dating, and then it's 6:50 and you're in love, and then it's seven o'clock and you're moving in together. If you hadn't broken your leg, you wouldn't be in love now.

I've been living my life stuck at six o'clock with the broken leg, stuck at *Dan's sick, and I'm gonna make him better.*

Well, I decide I'm moving up to seven! I'm going for the hawk's view. The full 360. I plan on landing on his ceiling and looking down on the entire scene.

Now there's almost a bounce in my step as I go from the dry bitter cold through the revolving glass doors and hit a solid wall of hospital heat.

On the elevator up, I feel different. I don't have the heavy heart and anxious anticipation that usually accompany me to the seventh floor. I have a sense of expectation. I am going to see something new. I am not going to see the tragedy that we've been living for sixteen years. There is another way of seeing it, and I am about to stand in a brand-new place in the middle of an old, old story.

What else is it? It's not just a tragedy. It's not just sad.

I walk into Dan's room. I stand at the foot of his bed, and I know for the first time, in the core of my being, that Dan is dying. Of course, I've known that for years. But this time, for the first time, there is no *resistance* in my knowing.

My son is dying. All these years, through all his brushes with death, his diabetic reactions, his close calls in hospitals, his airlifts to city hospitals, I knew Dan would die young, but I never believed he would actually die. How can a person hold two opposing truths with such steadfast resolve?

At that moment, something transcendent happens. It is a conversation that is not audible in the conventional sense. I hear it and I speak it, and I know without a shadow of a doubt that it is happening. But it is internal. I believe it to be a telepathic event. I am grateful that there even is a word for it. Otherwise I would not be able to put the experience into context. I know I am not making it up in a need for closure.

So here it is.

I am standing at the foot of Dan's bed and I say (only in my mind), *I know you are dying. I also know that what that really means is that you are going from form to formless. I get it. But I don't want our relationship to end. So can we make a deal that when you arrive wherever you are going, we can still communicate?*

Dan doesn't move. But then he hasn't moved for quite some time. I suggest some possibilities. I say, *Maybe every time I see a golden retriever, I will know it's you?* And then I think, *No, too common. Goldens are everywhere, and I can't expect you to be contacting me every minute.* I stand there in silence for a bit, and then I say (in my mind), *How about an exotic butterfly? Every time I see one, I'll know it's you.*

He is still staring at the ceiling with that horrible look on his face. I say (this is all still in my head), *No, that's no good either. Because then I'll barely ever see you. I'll think of something.*

And then his eyes move. The movement is so nuanced and minuscule that I think maybe I imagined it. But then a small grin forms on his lips, lips that have not changed for weeks. And then he says (remember, this is what I heard in my head), *Even in my death you're still trying to control me.*

Jesus, I know something huge has just transpired. We just communicated telepathically! Holy shit. I know this just happened. I'm not crazy. He just smiled!

Now here I am on center stage in my own play we call life, and I have to be in the balcony and be the witness. I have to be with Dan and have this extraordinary experience, and I also have to be in the audience and commit this to memory. I have to feel it from my guts, and I have to see it from a great distance. And I have to feel it from this close. And I have to see it from this far away. I know this is big. And I'm doing it. I'm making myself do it.

After a while, I move cautiously to the side of the bed, sure that if I make any abrupt movement it will break the spell and the only explanation I will end up with is wishful thinking and projection. I sit in the chair next to his head. And he starts to cough and then he starts to choke. Now that he has the trach, the phlegm buildup makes him gag and cough and choke, and it has to be suctioned out. Sarah, his girlfriend, and Joel have both learned how to do this. You have to clean your hands thoroughly, put on rubber gloves, rip open the package that includes all the parts you will need, loop up the suction catheter around your thumb, put your saline rinse bucket on his stomach for easy access, remove the oxygen tubing, insert the tube down his throat until there is resistance, and once he's coughing and choking, pull the catheter out and repeat.

I have tried and I have failed. I have not been able to look at his face desperately trying to get air. I just couldn't do it. I can't even watch when they do it. So when it's just Dan and me, I usually run out and get the respiratory nurse, who does the job. But this time while he is coughing and choking, something is telling me not to run and get the nurse. I don't understand how this is happening, but I get a clear message from Dan not to run for help, to let him do this himself. I sit there glued to the chair, watching him struggle and choke.

And all of a sudden, I get it. I say (in my head), *Dan, I never let you struggle. From the time you were a baby I jumped in every step of the way, keeping you from knowing your own strength, from finding out what you were made of. It was my fear, my inability to let go, to trust that your trip was your trip. So all your life I got between you and who you might have become. And now here at the end of your life, I finally get it. You can do this. Or you can't. But I can't save you anymore. I never should have kept trying. I should have trusted you, trusted that you could find your own power in yourself, your undeveloped self that I, in my terror, kept small.* And when I complete this thought, Dan, whose head has not moved in weeks, turns toward me! And the look of compassion that he gives me, the sweet understanding look of a wise and loving teacher, is something I will never forget. I can't remember exactly the words he uses, but it is something like *Good girl* or *Good for you. You finally got it.* And then a wink! I swear, a wink. And the words, better late than never. And then he smiles! I sit there in ecstasy.

Dan is sweating profusely. I am about to get a cloth to pat him down when my hands are suddenly not my own. They hover about six inches over Dan's chest, and then slowly they move in a parallel formation down the length of his body. I absolutely cannot put them down. An invisible force is keeping them up. It is as if someone else is moving them. When I get down to his feet, I make a cupping gesture, not at all something I would have known to do. My hands begin to travel up his body, moving the energy back up to his head. I say *moving the energy* because I can feel something resisting but not resisting so much that I can't move it.

I have been in the presence of energy healers, but I have never felt actual energy until this moment with Dan.

I move my hands over his body. I do this three times, and the last time his eyes close and his face looks relaxed and peaceful for the first time in weeks.

I sit down. Part of me knows that a miracle, something from the divine, has just happened and I should simply remain present. Another part of me wants to rush out into the night, grab my phone, and call Joel and tell him everything that has just transpired. *Why do you give everything away so fast?*

And then without thinking or warning, I am on my feet at the foot of his bed again. He is awake, and the frightened grimace has returned. And then a strange technicolor movie begins playing in my head. Puffy pink, baby-blue, pale-yellow, and white clouds surround a huge pewter gate. The doors open. I hear the words *Come, come, come*, and I know they are for Dan.

I am losing him. But when I look at my boy, the grimace is gone and his face is euphoric, filled with utter joy and disbelief.

A calm settles over us both. He continues to breathe softly. I sit in the dark in his room for a long while.

I have been grieving Dan for his whole life. What we have just done together will serve me for the rest of mine.

In the sixteen years that Dan has been sick, Joel has adapted every piece of equipment to fit his needs. He's built exercise bars, hung chains and hydraulic lifts. When Dan comes home from

Spaulding this last time, his intubation pump is so loud no one can hear anything but the roar and hiss of the machine.

Joel drives to the hardware store and returns with yards and yards of tubing. He works for five hours building a tunnel so that the noisy machine can be positioned outside Dan's room.

JOEL ARONIE: MIRACLE WORKER. I'll have business cards made.

I make the room beautiful. I buy him clothes that cover up the raw and red stoma sticking out of his lower abdomen. I dress him in big, floppy sweatshirts and baggy pants to disguise his stick-figure legs. And I coordinate the food. Joel and my good friend Gerry and I are a formidable team. Gerry does the psychological part and the musical part, Joel does the humor and the physical part, the lifting, the showering, and the making Dan laugh part.

I am still the Fixer. I still follow every lead of every possible cure. I reach Dan's old girlfriends and ask them to call him. I corral friends to come hang out for an hour here or an hour there. I lie in the bed next to him reading Peter Farrelly's book *Outside Providence*, everything George Carlin ever wrote, and Jean-Dominique Bauby's memoir, *The Diving Bell and the Butterfly*.

Joel has been sleeping next to Dan every night in his house in Vineyard Haven, and every night I go home to Chilmark, twenty minutes away, around 11:30.

On January 28, just before midnight, as I am leaving Dan's bedside, he signals that he wants to say something, that I should take the gauze off his throat. So I quickly wash my hands and put my finger over the hole, and he says clearly, almost loudly, "I love you, Mom."

Those are his last words to me.

On January 29, 2010, my star, my Danny boy, my supernova explodes and leaves us. Joel has just fallen asleep next to Dan when he takes his last breath. Josh, my older son, the most grounded human being I know, is there too. He says he heard a whoosh and felt something leave the room. I know that was Dan's gift to Josh.

One Saturday Joel and I are taking a walk when suddenly a huge flock of birds flies in that way they do, circling, dipping, rising, falling, and then landing on the telephone wires one by one, as if Michael Bennett himself had done the choreography on *A Chorus Line for Starlings*. The two of us gasp and watch as they swoop and dance. "How do they do that?" my husband says as they fly off, one by one, as if on cue. "One of them must say, 'OK, dudes, brunch at the Aronies', hit it.'" We laugh and then I say, "Is there any part of you that can imagine that Dan has something to do with this?"

My husband is a scientist. He doesn't shake his head or roll his eyes at me anymore. This marriage is many years old. He requires empirical proof to experience truth — and not of the woo-woo kind.

The birds continue their perfect performance, and my husband repeats: "How do they do that?"

And I hear from somewhere deep inside, "Tell him not to be so hung up on *how* it happened. Tell him better he should be blown away *that* it happened."

No goldens in sight. No exotic butterflies. Just dancing birds.

CHAPTER 69

Endings

Loose ends are exactly what they sound like, ends that have not been tied off, unfinished business.

Not every story has to have completion, but your main theme, your main reason for writing, has to be resolved or your reader will feel cheated. She'll feel cheated because you just cheated her.

You are not copying your journal entries. You are telling your story, showing your struggle, sharing your little victories and how you emerged out of the hole, only to be knocked back again, letting us climb out again and again with you. And ultimately giving us a map showing how you managed.

You're not recounting step by step exactly what you did but showing that it could be done. It was possible. That's all. That's it. Show me so I won't give up.

When your father dies in front of you and you're young, you have a few choices. One is, *Oh, look, unpredictable things can happen. I'll just be a leaf and let the wind decide where I'll land.* Or, as in my case, *This will never happen to me again. Never again will I suffer this much pain and shock. I will control everything and everyone. I'll make the leaves grow, and I'll decide when the wind will blow.*

During Dan's entire health journey, from nine months to thirty-eight years, I tried to control all the leaves on all the trees in all the lands. And nothing, including the wind, listened to me.

I think Dan consciously gave us our lives back. He knew we would have taken care of him until we were a hundred and ten. It would have been a privilege.

I remember feeding him one day about a year before he died.

He looked at me and said, "Mom, I wouldn't be alive if it weren't for you and Dad helping me." And then he got really quiet and he said, "But I hate being a burden."

I said, "You were a burden when you were an asshole. But now you're a gift."

As for the magic of our dear friend Gerry — Gerry who helped with the mortgage, Gerry who never tried to fix Dan, Gerry who helped me see the pathology of my relationship with Dan — coming into our lives when he did, who do I thank for that? I think of our alliance like a circle: no edges, pure elegance, perfect balance. Everybody got what they needed. Gerry needed family. We gave him one. He loved Dan, and Dan loved him back. I needed a shrink, a mentor. And Joel needed, as he confided to me recently, help and support with his wife, Intense Nancy, and having Gerry there was like having a relief pitcher.

Five years after Dan died, we bought a little black Miata convertible on eBay. Now we drive to Aquinnah, the westernmost point on the island, with the top down, sometimes even when it's cold. We sing songs from *The Pajama Game*. Or something from *Guys and Dolls*, or we listen to Jack Kornfield.

And we thank Dan.

We drive to a few of his favorite fishing spots, and we park and cry and reminisce and cry some more. And then one of us says, "Slow down, Turbo," or, "Not too shabby," or, "I definitely don't want to give up and die horny." And there he is, with us, again and always. Just in a different form.

Joel and I agree, as weird as it might sound, that Dan was happiest the last few years of his life. The Surrendered Years. Even though I had all the spiritual words for surrender, the actual act, the letting go, the no need to control *anything*, evaded me for a long time. But I did it. I slowly made my way across the narrow divide and joined Dan and Joel and Josh, who had been waiting for me. The overpass had a blinking neon sign that read Acceptance.

Prompt

Go buy a copy of this book for your best writer friend. ☺

Acknowledgments

I wish to thank the six midwives without whom this book would never have been born: Suzy Becker, Connie Berry, Carol Gilligan, Judy Hannan, Dede Lahman, and Jan Winburn.

Thank you to my brilliant editors, Jason Gardner, Kristen Cashman, and Mimi Kusch. And to my friend and agent, Flip Brophy. And thanks to Wally Lamb, who never says no to me.

My gratitude to my writing group, who are my muses every Tuesday at 4:00 (depending on who's in Ireland and who's not): Jamie Kageleiry, Nicole Galland, Laura Roosevelt, Kate Feiffer, Cathy Walthers, Lara O'Brien, and Melissa Hackney.

My love and appreciation to my early readers: Howard Wells, Jody Hefren, Arnie Reisman, Paula Lyons, Bob Brustein and Doreen Beinhart, Sig Van Raan and Susan Dickler, Denise Barach, Bhavani Nelson, Kay Goldstein, and Frannie Southworth. To Pete and Seven, who continue to print on demand.

And to the friends who have held me and fed me: Lorie and Richard Hamermesh, Jane Lancellotti, Jacqueline Vischer, John Zeisel, Brooke Adams, Tony Shalhoub, Judith Kaufman, Steve Kemper, Sharon and David Mann, Jamie Hamlin, Margot Datz, Carol and George Brush, Gerry and Martha Yukevich, Susie Oken, Margaret and Gerry Storrow, Niki Patton, Merle and David Trager, Nancy Berger, Elise LeBovit, Steven and Judith Kampman, Angel Shepard, Saundra Hart-LaBelle, Louise Kennelley, Shaunan Trollson, Barbara Edelstein, Debbie Phillips, Kathy Olsen, Charlie Hoye, Becky Minnick, and Dylan and Connor Beeson. Thank you to the whole West Meadow clan: Brook and Michael Urban, Jane Rainwater and Ed Hogan, Julie Hauserman, John Cooney, and Malachy Duffy.

And to my Connecticut family: Aunt Shirley Wachtel, Stu and Sue Wachtel, Ted Wachtel, Deb and Chris Chessari, and my brother, Ron Curtis.

And with undying love and forever gratitude to my two constant spirit guides: my sister, Frances Slonim Curtis Barnhart, and my son Dan. And my Hennie, the best mother a daughter could have.

To my sister's three babies: Adam Curtis, Jennifer Prax, and Elizabeth Moss.

To every Aronie everywhere, Michale and Emmanuel and Aprill.

And my precious Aronie brothers, Al, Steve, and Mart.

And thank you to the Universe, which keeps saying yes to me.

Publication Credits

Material from certain chapters was previously published in an earlier form in the following publications.

Blue Dot Living: Chapter 23.
Martha's Vineyard Times: Chapters 6, 16, 20, 28, 49, and 53.
Moment magazine: Chapter 66.
MAX magazine: Chapter 67.
National Public Radio: Chapters 45, 67, and 68.
Northeast Magazine (Hartford Courant): Chapters 30 and 31.
Vineyard Gazette: Chapters 4, 7, and 10.

Material from the following chapters is from the author's unpublished memoir: Chapters 10, 11, 17, 18, and 21.

About the Author

Nancy Slonim Aronie is the founder of the Chilmark Writing Workshop on Martha's Vineyard and author of *Writing from the Heart: Tapping the Power of Your Inner Voice*. She was a commentator for National Public Radio's *All Things Considered* and a visiting writer at Trinity College in Hartford, Connecticut. Aronie wrote a monthly column in *McCall's* magazine and was a recipient of the Eye of the Beholder Artist in Residence Award at the Isabella Stewart Gardner Museum in Boston. She was recognized for excellence in teaching for all three years she taught with Robert Coles at Harvard University. Aronie teaches Jump-Start Your Memoir and Write It from the Heart at Esalen Institute, Kripalu Center for Yoga and Health, Omega Institute, New York Open Center, and Blue Spirit Costa Rica. Her column "From the Heart" appears biweekly in the *Martha's Vineyard Times*.